THE
PARTING
YEARS
1963-74

Cecil Beaton's Diaries
Volume Six

SAPERE
BOOKS

THE
PARTING
YEARS
1963-74

Published by Sapere Books.

11 Bank Chambers, Hornsey, London, N8 7NN,
United Kingdom

saperebooks.com

ISBN: 978-1-912546-43-5

Foreword to the New Edition

I welcome the republication of the six volumes of Cecil Beaton's diaries, which so delighted readers between 1961 and 1978. I don't know if Cecil himself re-read every word of his manuscript diaries when selecting entries, but I suspect he probably did over a period of time. Some of the handwritten diaries were marked with the bits he wanted transcribed and when it came to the extracts about Greta Garbo, some of the pages were sellotaped closed. Even today, in the library of St John's College, Cambridge, some of the original diaries are closed from public examination, though to be honest, most of the contents are now out in the open.

The only other person who has read all the manuscript diaries is me. It took me a long time to get through them, partly because his handwriting was so hard to read. I found that if I read one book a day, I had not done enough. If I did two in a day, then I ended up with a splitting headache! This in no way deflected from the enormous enjoyment in reading them.

Altogether there are 145 original manuscript diaries dating from Cecil going up to Cambridge in 1922 until he suffered a serious stroke in 1974. A few fragments of an earlier Harrow diary survive, and there is a final volume between 1978 and 1980, written in his left hand. 56 of these cover his time at Cambridge, some of which appear in *The Wandering Years* (1961). 22 books cover the war years, and were used for *The Years Between* (1965), and nine books record his *My Fair Lady* experiences, some of which appear in *The Restless Years* (1976) and were the basis for *Cecil Beaton's Fair Lady* (1964). These six volumes probably represent about ten per cent of what Cecil Beaton actually wrote.

The diaries attracted a great deal of attention when first published. James Pope-Hennessy wrote of Cecil's 'thirst for self-revelation', adding that the unpublished volumes were surely 'the chronicle of our age'. Referring to Cecil's diaries, and those of Eddy Sackville-West, he also commented: 'We could not be hoisted to posterity on two spikier spikes.'

I have to tell the reader that these volumes were not always quite the same as the originals. Some extracts were rewritten with hindsight, some entries kaleidoscoped and so forth. Certain extracts in these six volumes were slightly retouched in places, in order that Cecil could present his world to the reader exactly as he wished it presented. And none the worse for that.

Hugo Vickers

January 2018

Part I: Home and Away, 1963-4

RETURN TO AN OLD HAUNT

London: December 1963

Visited D. Bryce Smith's artist's materials shop in the Hampstead Road, a haunt of my extreme youth. This Euston neighbourhood, once flourishing, in a small Dickensian way, is now in the throes of a huge reconstruction; there are to be overpasses, underpasses, garages and skyscrapers. Meanwhile, little derelict shops are to be pulled down. My old 'Aladdin's Cave' of hot-pressed and rice-paper notebooks still survives, with a lease of ten years to go, but all around is decay. Shades of Eggie Hine at Harrow, my first Diaghilev ballet sketches, and Pavlova drawn on rice-leaf pages. This is where I used to come to get the tools of my trade.

It was depressing to come back. So much was 'no longer available'. Cox's rough paper gone; so much that was of quality now superseded. An arty-genteel lady served me in an almost deserted shop in which a few slipshod, makeshift partitions were hiding the living quarters backstage. There were heavy layers of dust on old notebooks on shelves and, on the counter, hideous, garish calendars and gimmicky, trashy gadgets. The arty lady saw I wanted a lot of things but was easily diverted to gossip over the telephone when it rang.

I kept ordering in vast quantities, inspired by the thought that there was much to design in the near future (*Traviata*, *Arabella*, the Lerner musical about Chanel). I was refusing to be daunted by the unhelpfulness of the arty lady, or by the difficulty of getting what I really wanted.

I went out hopefully with papers and notebooks under my arm, but hardly with the elation in my heart that I had had when I was twenty.

December 11th, 1963

Exercises at eight o'clock were quite an effort with a hangover. Decided to give up work for the day. Lunch with Patrick Plunket. Highly sophisticated fish food at Wilton's, served as in a nursery. Jokes, high spirits, followed by tour to Bond Street; strange frantic shoppers; on to crowded David Hockney exhibition. He is undoubtedly an original, and his engravings for *Rake's Progress* are beautiful. This Manchester boy with the yellow glasses, yellow dyed hair and exaggerated north-country accent was accosted at vernissage by an irate lady. In a loud voice she challenged him for drawing his nude women in such a distorted manner. 'Can you really imagine that is the way the arm comes out of the socket? Look at their bosoms — they're nowhere near where they should be. Have you ever seen a naked woman?' 'A dorn't knogh ars ah harve!' 'Well, I'll tell you the hips are not like that; the *entrejamb* starts here, not there. The thighs aren't flat like that, the buttocks aren't small and squashed and sideways. Don't you realize that the rib cage runs down to the groin?' 'A dorn't knogh ars ahm unturusted!'

Highly civilized evening with Bertie Abdy. He formed collections for Chester Beatty and for Gulbenkian, and had close connections with Wildenstein. When he bought a Renoir for five thousand francs he was called a '*milord-imbécile*' in the French press for doing so. He had the first exhibition of Paul Klee, and although the highest price was £14 he did not sell one. An art connoisseur *par excellence*, but who must make money, he has now fallen on better days, comparatively.

Jane Abdy in black organza from Dior. Best Rothschild wine and food. Felt utterly at ease, loving every rare moment of Bertie's fascinating stories of the dishonesty of art dealers. Of course Bertie always does the best for himself, and has the whole world of art dealers against him. But they know he has an eye and knowledge, and they are terrified of him.

Fascinating conversation with Edwina d'Erlanger who relishes the luxurious nuances of clocks and Chinese china. Edwina added her experience of nearly being swindled out of £10,000 over a pair of pearl earrings.

December 19th

Brando Brandolini and Cristiana were being entertained at the David Somersets, so not only did I throw myself joyously into the atmosphere of cigar smoke and Dom Perignon gaiety, but after two hours went on to a young beatnik party given by Lucy Lambton for Michael Wishart.

Reddish: December 21st

Crichel came to lunch. The 'boys'[1] are all elderly men now. Eddie, a lord, cannot and need not work. His taxes make it simpler not to earn. Desmond Shawe-Taylor exploded with rage when I asked if he'd approve of a *Traviata* country scene taking place in a stable. 'You can't write notes in a stable — she's got to have a desk.' His eyes shot red flames. I felt unable to concentrate upon Trevor-Roper's diagnosis of imaginary or non-imaginary pains as I was too busy clearing the table, and with the dining-room reverberating more than I realized, I found myself hard of hearing and sadly missed a lot of the

---

[1] Raymond Mortimer, Eddie Sackville-West (Lord Sackville), Patrick Trevor-Roper, and Desmond Shawe-Taylor share a house at Crichel in Dorset.

conversation on the subject of Stephen Tennant's eccentricity and young Julian Jebb's longing to make the pilgrimage to his house at Wilsford.

An afternoon walk started aimlessly but gained impetus. It was such a cold afternoon that we had to be brisk. A round, rose-coloured sun was fast sinking, the rolling hills in the distance sweet-pea coloured, the ground beneath one hard as crystal. The pigs were eating the wooden stanchions of their sties. The calves very somnolent; the birds, few left behind, flying off straight to the horizon. Walked over crusty, ploughed fields, over the hill above Broadchalke, then down the avenue of elms where I exerted myself, 'doing a Queen Mary', pulling the ivy off the trunks, a miniscule contribution but utterly absorbing. Glowing with health I returned to the village where the local children were coming out of the hall having seen *Treasure Island*. I went to the church to look at the chair given in memory of my mother, but found the door locked.

STAYING WITH MICHAEL DUFF AT VAYNOL

Christmas Day, 1963
Mount Snowdon visible — sunny — the wind dropped and temperature mounted.

I remember many nice Christmases here in the past. Fancy dresses, charades, huge breakfast table, present-giving. Juliet Duff, Nora Lindsay, Tilly Losch, Oggie Lynn, Micky Renshaw, etc. Now this year my stomach put a damper on everything. I felt rather appalled at the kilos of kaolin which were not drowning the pains. However, I was lucky to be able to spend most of the day in bed without feeling that I was being a nuisance. There are twenty-eight people in this house, servants included. Everyone giving each other presents makes a mountain of wastepaper. I was bidden to come down for the ceremony. Our names on chairs and tables at appropriate places. Michael's book on Tutankhamun, and a blue tie from Laura were my nicest presents. Mine weren't bad to Diana, so appreciative of her Floris. All the children and nannies come down for lunch. Balloons whizzing through the air as they were burst.

The visit of the carollers was a delight, with bishop, accordion player, lanterns, and sheets of music. They made a pretty picture in the stuccoed hall in their red caps and cassocks and white ruffs; men's hands shrouded in thick gloves. They sang in English, though they are more at home in Welsh, and finished the cycle with 'Silent Night'. More carols on the television after dinner. We watched and listened to the marvellous sounds coming from King's College, Cambridge. The faces of these boys are as extraordinarily fine and untrammelled as their voices.

MOUTON

January 1964

To defile, even by lying against them, the exquisitely embroidered linen pillows, was the greatest luxury. My bedroom, the Persian room, was small but comfortable. There were baskets by the bedside with sharpened pencils and rulers. There was a half-bottle of whisky, with a half-bottle of Perrier and ice in case one needed a refresher. On the rim of the bath there was a frilled lamp by which one could read, and a row of Floris scents, violet, gardenia, etc. The linen was impeccable. Every detail perfection in its finish. Pauline Rothschild, alone, could have arranged the still-life of bottles, the pots of green plants, and the white hyacinths.

It appears that to run this house in this prodigious way takes Pauline one and three-quarters to two hours each day; she has an immediate post-mortem with the chef as soon as possible after every meal. Pauline is someone of fable, entirely dedicated to the arts but with her head sufficiently balanced to know exactly how she can achieve this dream.

Dinner was the best of all, as Philippe agreed — *moule* soup (flavoured with curry) in small Russian cups, flaming quails, *pâté de foie* — the best, pinkest and freshest — and a sorbet, or lemon ice-cream, of a cornflour texture with the slightest suggestion of lemon rind. Perfection! As for the wines, Cyril Connolly remembers that they were historic. He lifted his glass to his nose and said: 'We are drinking something that hardly exists anywhere any more. This is very rare.' He savoured the wine to the full.

Cyril has a reputation for being a glutton. But this is not fair. He did not overeat this weekend. He knows when it is time to say 'no more'. He is too much of an artist to gorge himself and there is something very appealing and touching about his restraint.

He likes food perhaps more than anyone I know, but that is rather another mark in his favour. Good food does not necessarily have to be rich. I asked Deirdre Connolly if she cooked well. Cyril, most loyal, in front of the Rothschild panoply, interpolated: 'Yes, very. She makes me the most delicious dinners and often brings them in on a tray in front of the fire. There is a wonderful fish shop in Seaford, an excellent fruiterer in Eastbourne, and a marvellous butcher that we motor over to in Lewes....'

Then completely unsnobbish, Cyril brought out a present for Philippe. From a crumpled brown paper-bag he produced some Cox's Orange Pippins. He shook them against his ear to hear if they rattled. 'Yes, they're ripe. Try this one. There's a very good fruit shop at Victoria Station.'

January 14th

My sixtieth birthday. Pleasant, quiet morning; no particular pain at such a ruthless reminder that I'm getting old. I don't mind the closer proximity to death, but I hate the degeneration in mind and body. The spirit is as young as it was, but it's sad that I don't seem to *develop*.

February 9th

Simon Fleet had arranged a pub crawl of the East End, a dozen of us in three cars; a Chinese restaurant; only faintly amusing *décor* in the pubs; amazing to see the prosperity of the dockers, all well dressed, wearing starched collars and blue suits. The beat-look out. Dancing the Shake; no one minding anything or anybody.

The real thrill was seeing the Christopher Wren house at midnight on Cardinal's Wharf. This exquisite tall grey-stone house looks on to a miraculous view of the river, with barges beached at low ride and hazy St Paul's in the distance. The monochrome scene of liquid lights, black cranes, silver and mist, was unbelievably mysterious and romantic.

A pity I see so little of this part of London which has a historical grandeur completely lacking in the bourgeois prettiness of Kensington.

ST MORITZ

March 1st

The first days were a bit of an anxiety. Although the chalet is enormous, with an army of servants to attend one's every wish, the life is foreign to one's own. The ways had to be learnt. Others were so expert at them that I felt a bit like a new boy at boarding school.

There was a slight feeling of impending doom, no doubt exaggerated by the climate. The mountains were enveloped in mist, the snow very patchy.

The fact that the sun was hidden in the clouds robbed the place of much of its charm. To begin with I wondered if I would be able to stick a week of this, then suddenly the sun came out. All was changed under a blue sky. The newly fallen snow was crisp. One's spirits rose, morbidity vanished. The routine of easy living enveloped one completely.

It is only after several days that one realizes how healthy the life is. There is the temptation to drink too much, yet the air is doing its good work all the time. By degrees one feels that the lack of responsibility, and the inability to write even a letter, is all part of a cure that will benefit one later.

The laughs, the wit, the gaiety and the parties are entertaining, the luxury extraordinary. There is everything, yet there is something missing, and that is a basic simplicity. Also I feel the need of someone to talk to with whom I have more in common.

Frivolity is fine. I am good at throwing in the witty phrase, at getting a laugh. I enjoy developing this, and it amazes me sometimes how glib and expert my facility is. But I have always felt the need of a guy-rope, someone who can help me retain some discipline, who can perhaps enjoy some of the frivolities but who will help me to stop short as soon as they become too suffocating.

March 2nd

My friend, Lilia Ralli, was staying nearby. She talked of Charles Bestigui's eccentricity. Whatever the cause, he gives his old friends hell. His smart acquaintances now leave him to his crotchety vagaries. It seems that recently Ode de Munn's dog, Capucine, died. Charles hated the dog yet built it a Nelson's column memorial in the park at Groussay. Ode, appalled by such hypocrisy, wanted her dog buried in her own garden, so she sent a boot box filled with trash for Charles to inter at the base of the column.

Charles is now selling up the Palazzo Labia (he could well afford to give it as a great gesture to the city of Venice) and is building more and more in the park at Groussay which, with Danish gazebo, Chinese bridge and Portuguese pavilions, resembles the World's Fair.

Now that he cannot walk, he is determined that his friends shall also ride in hand carriages, and so he employs beplumed and titivated negro boys to do the pushing.

AUDREY HEPBURN

Leaving St Moritz for Lucerne

The day of our departure was bright. The scenery from the train windows was very beautiful as the pine trees, freshly cushioned with snow, passed in a pageant of silver, white and black. The crystal lights on the new-fallen snow added an extra texture. The mountains were spiky and hard against the blue sky. The train circled down, until eventually there was no more snow and in the orchards the labourers were pruning the fruit trees, leaving a bird's nest of branches beneath each tree trunk. What satisfaction in six months' time when they come home late in the evening with their carts piled high with the fruit.

The mood of slight foreboding that I am apt to feel in high mountains, and certainly experienced on the dark, cloudy days in St Moritz, gave way to one of joy and freedom on arrival in Lucerne. Medieval and eighteenth-century buildings clustered at the edge of Lake Lucerne, interspersed with avenues of pollarded trees; long bridges spanned the water. Here were dozens of church steeples, tall and more pointed than usual, and here were real shops with real books and Picasso postcards, and the best linen and watches. Audrey and Mel Ferrer were in good spirits: 'We'll be there with bells on,' Audrey had said, and they were. They took me to a tea house where the people behind the counter were happy to serve us; where we met with the solicitude that has been a feature since the Kaiser came here at the end of last century but which has been missing in other parts of the world.

Motoring along the lake to their Burgenstock chalet in the mountains on the other side of the lake, I had a glimpse of the country that I love: woods and orchards, and cottages with gardens. We came to a strange group of Edwardian hotels owned by Audrey and Mel's landlord and, it now being out of season, they had a strange Thomas Mann, deserted quality; but not so my friends' little wooden chalet. This was brimming over with the delightful, smiling Italian and Swiss servants who had tended Audrey and Mel so well in Hollywood; and here was Sean, their son, redcheeked and thrilled, shouting a welcome.

To step inside this Swiss doll's house was to realize what I had missed in St Moritz. Everything was white, and of a clean simplicity; white cotton covers on chairs, long white net curtains and white Swiss linen everywhere; huge bouquets of white tulips or yellow flowers to complement the orange and yellow sofas; an incredible impeccability — in the modern white china, the embroidered napkin wrapping the brown-bread toast, the array of books, the Picasso drawing, the Modigliani figure, the Matisse head. The bedrooms with their covers and huge pillows were of a mountain-water cleanliness. This was something more nourishing that a good steak, for it was food for the spirit.

Audrey is a natural. She has taken up her role in life with a complete ease that is rare. She is strong and firm in character, and seems to be never swayed to do the foolish or unkind thing. Her relationship with Mel is not all that easy, but she loves him. Audrey takes the rough with the smooth and there is a great deal of the smooth. Her success is astonishing and not only financially. Yet she never allows herself to regard it except as her professional career; it comes second to her private life.

Audrey is very proud of her home and everything in it. The evening meal is the great food event of the day. Audrey takes pains over the artichokes, Roman-style (basted in butter and parsley), the beef with carrots, the Swiss *pâtisseries*. The infinite trouble and the finesse she manages strike me as being extraordinary.

New York: March

Halfway across the Atlantic, Pelham Place had receded into the distance and the readjustment to New York had started.

The arrival had its own character. A man from the Metropolitan Opera House met me with a car, and gave me good news of the production of *La Traviata* that I was to work on. Messages had been left for me at the hotel, and before I had unpacked an excited Alfred Lunt was on the line. Could we go immediately to the opera house? Before many minutes in the company of Krawitz, Wrong and Bing, my colleagues in this venture, I began to feel I had always been there. The old problems arose; not much money; little rehearsal time; and too many productions in too short a time. But

Alfred, smelling of beer, said his piece, and apologized for talking too much. He is sweet and understanding and a good man, and I pray to God that I will always love him. Alfred took me home in the afternoon but I was too keyed up and exhausted to sleep. At eight o'clock I went to the dinner he and Lynn were giving for me. Truman was there, the Joe Alsops, Madeleine Sherwood and others, and soon I was involved in local gossip.

Truman came back with me to the hotel. We talked over whiskies and sodas until I realized that by English time it was 7.30 in the morning.

When I woke I spoke for one hour on the telephone to Diana Vreeland. She inspired me, and gave me impetus to carry me through my non-stop day. Diana has learnt not to be pressurized. She's never in a hurry, though she knows there are dozens of people waiting for her to hang up the receiver.

Lunch at the Met., followed by Zefferelli's *Falstaff*, then, in the evening, *Dolly* with Margaret Case. To end the day, a snowstorm. It gave us such a surprise when we came out of the theatre and prevented our finding a cab. So we had to trudge through the tornado and were soaked through by the time we got back to the hotel.

Stratford: April

To Stratford to see the exhibition celebrating the quatercentenary of Shakespeare's birth. This proved to be Dickie Buckle's triumph! Absolutely thrilling, mysterious, surprising, shocking, full of contrasts; and, above all, imaginative. Pop art and Nicholas Hilliard, rare Elizabethan revelry and modern junk; music, sonnets, and scent coming out of the ethos to greet one. The Elizabethan London of Timothy O'Brien evoked in terms of today; Elizabeth being cheered as she passed in her chair the burnt corpses of the plague; among the squalor, a huge hunk of bleeding meat hanging in mid-air. Alan Tagg's work was subtle and sensitive; a long gallery of authentic Elizabethan portraits and a clever, fascinating model of the Globe Theatre. The Jean Hugo murals were old fashioned but, I suppose, a good contrast.

At the theatre there was a marvellous production of *Richard II*. All the actors in this company have a mastery of style, a reverence for the poetry and none of the ranting of the old ham. David Warner's interesting portrayal of Richard II was off-hand, and his obsequious attitude utterly contemporary. I felt Stratford as alive as in Shakespeare's day, and the spirit of the bard strongly in my bones.

The first photographs of Prince Edward: May

From the moment the group assembled themselves in the white oasis in front of the camera, the pattern seemed to form and the lighting proved as luminous as we had hoped. Moreover, the infant showed *bonhomie* and an interest in the activity that was going on. His behaviour pleased and amused the Queen, who was in a happy, contented and calm mood, and smilingly obeyed my instructions.

Prince Andrew was determined to be in every picture, and behaved like a professional, adding the charm of the too-young-to-know-really-what-it-is-all-about.

I found myself rushing up and down a step-ladder with the celerity of a mountain goat. The Queen remarked on the speed with which I cranked the camera: 'He's much quicker than I am!' I noted that sweat was running down my torso. But such effort was justified. Sometimes I click with desperate speed, hoping that some fluke will evolve. This time I felt that good results were being got immediately. The Queen's wide grin dominated the picture, and other felicitous elements were provided by Andrew's blue, wistful, little-boy eyes and those of the infant who was alert, curious, and already a character.

The day was dark and grey, with lowering clouds, but there was enough light and we moved to take pictures around the crib in which the Queen, Princess Margaret and all her children had lain. Thence to the blue porphyry columns, and to the blue brocaded drawing-room next door. These pictures were more banal, but I was elated at having chosen white-paper backgrounds, as the gilt and heavy marble columns, though impressive to the eye, have been overdone and appear fussy and old-fashioned.

Andrew, the dominant figure, remained cheerful, the baby continued to hold its own, and each time I asked the Queen if she had had enough, she was *just* willing to continue a little longer. 'Look his eyelashes are all tangled!' she said, admiring the latest addition to the family. 'It's most unfortunate that all my sons have such long eyelashes while my daughter hasn't any at all.'

May

I seldom notice the presence of Mrs Cartwright, who has been a faithful member of the Pelham Place entourage for many years now. She is quiet and tactful, and although I try to treat her as a human-being I am generally so absorbed in writing a letter or choosing the best poses out of a hundred negatives while she is tidying the room, that there is seldom more than a cursory exchange of politenesses. Mrs Cartwright is rather shy and tentative. Only once did she overcome her reserve: she tried to comfort me when I was sitting at my desk convulsed with tears at hearing the news that Peter Watson had been drowned.

I have heard, through Eileen,[2] that Mrs Cartwright has strong dislikes. At one time she got on extremely badly with Cornelius, the cook; although she has a bawdy sense of humour she can be easily shocked, as when she saw a set of nude photographs I'd taken and covered them up as they lay on my desk.

Eileen, arriving in my bedroom at the start of another busy day, is always treated to a short account of the previous evening's happenings before the telephone interrupts us, and the awful, harrowing, unnerving rush to get to my first appointment starts.

My dinner party had portended well. I had brought up from the country, with great care, three beautiful bottles of rare claret — Rothschild 1928 and 1921. These were for the benefit of Cyril Connolly who was coming to London in order to have dinner with me. I had invited Cyril and his wife, Deirdre, Bertie and Jane Abdy, and Martita Hunt. But I had to confess to Eileen that although the intentions of the guests were friendly, the atmosphere had been indefinably spiky. I did not quite know why, but neither the Connollys nor the Abdys seemed to be playing on my side. Maybe it was my imagination, but Cyril seemed aggressive; perhaps it was his way of trying to cover up the lateness of their arrival. No sooner had he appeared than he was baiting Bertie, who was fatuously 'poohpoohing' Cézanne and saying his importance was only fabricated by women and dealers; Bertie's theories about nobody caring about art, only about the money that art can provide, become more ridiculous.

---

[2] Eileen Hose, my friend and secretary.

Bertie then said to me: 'May I be perfectly frank? I don't think you should have these rugs on this lovely floor. You should get rid of them.'

Talk had been so intelligent that later Martita told me she had not felt equal to joining in. However, she did hold forth later on as a connoisseur of food, and where to get the best in London. This she did with consummate style and she displayed her flair and taste in the way that justified her presence.

A day later Eileen arrived in the country. As we sat in the drawing-room after dinner, she said: 'You know, you were right about what you said about your dinner party not being quite easy. Mrs Cartwright had noticed it, and told me all about it. She said that she sensed it from the moment the Abdys arrived and Sir Robert asked her, it being quite a lovely summer evening, "Are we dining in the garden?"' Upon entering the drawing-room he had asked me the same question in a rather bullying tone. I could not remember my reply, but Mrs Cartwright had and had thought it was rather good: 'No, and I'm afraid it's too late to get a nightingale from Berkeley Square.'

Unaware to me, Mrs Cartwright had gone back to Streatham with her head full of interesting impressions of an evening that I knew was not at all cosy, yet which, but for her, would soon have been forgotten.

A TOUR OF ENGLAND

June 1964

I was glad England had played up and presented a high-summer evening of perfect beauty. The roses were billowing in every Great Western Road villa garden. Kin's[3] reactions, as

[3] My good friend, Kinmont Trefry Hoitsma from San Francisco.

usual, were very much to the point. I could hardly imagine that the plans had worked so well — touch wood. We motored to Pelham, talking hard — so much to laugh about. First he must see his room. Was the bed too small? His legs hung way out over the end. But perhaps we could arrange something else. 'Have you had dinner?' 'Yes, but you know me.' He ate a second one, and then in the twilight we drove through London to the City to see St Paul's, the Monument, Wren churches; then through Covent Garden and the Strand, St James's Park, the Mall, past St James's Palace. I talked continuously and Kin was asleep. (He had not slept for two nights.) Then, back home, he slept the sleep of the dead. This difficult, strangely untrained, yet high-quality American had seen fit to give himself into my trust, and accept my offer to make a new life for him over here.

In the glorious sun of Tuesday we set out in the car for Land's End, the first leg of a voyage to see my own country, a journey that was to take us all over the kingdom. The West was beautiful in spite of the first rush of holidaymakers, and 'Bed and Breakfast' signs were everywhere.

Exeter Cathedral, more squat than Salisbury, but original and successful, with a frieze of carvings on the façade. No room at the first inn; a hideous dinner at a restaurant; the night spent at a soulless motel. But what does it matter if our spirits are high and our affections involved.

Land's End, its rugged, clean, primeval beauty unsullied by the press of trippers; St Michael's Mount; the Headland Hotel at Newquay, a red brick Victorian monstrosity gloriously perched above ocean and rock. A trio played excruciatingly during dinner; typically bad English fare with mayonnaise out of a bottle.

Early dawn departure; enough of Cornwall. The huge hedges prevent one seeing the glorious views except when going down steep hills. (Thank heavens for our well-cut hedgerows in Wiltshire.) After the winding roads of Cornwall we found it was possible to make good time. We went back through Exeter, and then on to Glastonbury Abbey. Kin liked this very much. He leapt about, taking many photographs with real enthusiasm. The monk's kitchen, a tall white circular room, was, he said, the sort of room he would like to live in.

The high-summer weather had gone as suddenly as it arrived, and now all was cold and grey. Wells Cathedral did not look its best. It has a certain character but is not really impressive as a creative expression of devotion.

Saturday, July 11th

We went to Coventry to see the cathedral there. On second sight it is more impressive, especially now that the crowds have diminished. Piper's and other stained-glass windows theatrical, and the modern architecture of 'explosive forms' interesting, as are the modern cross and sculptures in side chapels. Very moving the remains of the bombed cathedral with the burnt-out cross on the altar and the words — 'Forgive them for what they did ...' or some such inscription. The tapestry designed by Graham Sutherland is a miracle of the weaver's art.

Then to Derby, and soon signposts to Kedleston. It was not open to the public but I bluffed lodgekeepers and drove into a glorious park with a lake and up to the bolted front door. In the church nearby a hilarious marble monument of Lord Curzon and his first wife lying side by side. She was the Chicago heiress whose mother said at the time of the engagement: 'Mr Leiter has been so generous to Mary, he's given her *bête noire* for her trousseau.'

Miles covered early — too soon to arrive at Chatsworth, so first to Haddon Hall. In the chapel, which has beautiful frescoes in black and white linear designs, is Violet, Duchess of Rutland's effigy of her nine-year-old son — a triumph for someone who had previously done no sculpture — a *tour de force* of emotion. Kin deeply roused by beauty of long room, the terraces with buttresses from which trees grew, the rivers and streams gushing, the herds wallowing in daisies; the Elizabethan rose-gardens, and the kitchens, where Kin's imagination worked overtime conjuring up the rush and bustle of dozens of cooks preparing enormous meals; the brown and oatmeal-coloured wood worn by use and polished like glass.

Thence to Chatsworth. In Debo's absence, Emma and her new husband[4] were hosts, and very accommodating and interesting on their own.

Kin overjoyed and laughing at the grandeur of Chatsworth bedroom — the windows soaring for ever — my bed with gilded dome reminded him, with its ruched silk, of a funeral casket.

Emma told us that the government had taken seven priceless works of art from the collection at Chatsworth to pay for death duties; an early Greek head, a missal of infinite value, a Holbein cartoon of Henry VIII, rare books, and, she added, 'then they took Hardwick'. We visited Hardwick the next day, a house built by the energetic Bess who hankered for light, hence windows everywhere, miles of them; a wonderful gallery; wide staircases and landings; needlework and heraldic animals.

Sightseeing by the mile at Chatsworth: signs of untold wealth even after the government *did* pick the cherries. Details strike a

---

[4] The Duchess of Devonshire's daughter and her husband Toby Tennant.

note of luxury — the window panes of bevelled glass, windows lined with gold; masterpieces of painting tucked in a corner. Halcyon weather; idyllic parkland and situation. Telescopic lens of camera trained on distances and Japanesey bridges, spires of model village church, a Greek statue rose-clung.

Through the fumes of surrounding smoking mines, we visited Sutton Scarsdale, a sad ruin, bought hopelessly by Osbert Sitwell; nothing can be done with it now; too expensive to build and no land; not even romantic. On to Bolsover, a marvellous ruin, with square patches of sunlight on clipped lawns through empty windows. Impressive dormer-window embellishments.

Leeds, Sheffield, the smoking chimneys, wires, derricks, cranes. The clustered villages on slopes of moors, the drab symmetry of slum roads, dark brick walls, mauve-painted doors. The young men of the towns are 'beat' in appearance. The population doomed to live here and not liking it any more than I do. Kin understands them. They like the cinema and know it is an expression of art, an artificial form. They like their families, music; they read, they have immortal longings.

The soot gave way to moors, with bracken and huge oak forests and we were in the West Riding.

For our first glimpse of it the Lake District — Ullswater, Windermere — was at its most calendar-art picturesque, but this did not detract in any way from beauty on such a scale. Gentian and periwinkle mountains, new-lettuce-green trees, waterfalls, glassy smooth lakes; pine trees, sheep, bracken. The air so clear.

We photographed, we walked, we watched sheep shearing, we thrust our noses into hay-barns and were euphoric about the smells. Goats and sheep were bleating, turkeys gobbling, doves cooing.

Stopping to telephone our progress to the Sekers' household, the 1850 hotel struck one as being so much cleaner than elsewhere.

A warm welcome from Miki Sekers, dressed like an old-fashioned circus proprietor off duty, in jersey, Ascot stock and loose trousers — Hungarian high spirits and hospitality. Open house. Nice intelligent son David and young men from the mill. Paprika chicken. Dom Perignon champagne. Luxury — success — money easy — laughter easy — friendship easy. Late-Georgian house decorated as if by Gladys Calthrop for the latest Noël Coward drawing-room comedy — a Monet, Bonnards, Sutherlands, mixed with Victorian junk. No restraint here.

The glorious weather had given place to rain, but perhaps it was right that we should see this district at its most typical. Miki, early in my room, provided a type-written itinerary with suggestions for our day's jaunt to Cockermouth, Keswick, Penrith, Appleby and Temple Sowerby.

At Temple Sowerby we find on the green in front of the maypole a charming, minute house called The Cedars, where my mother had lived as a child. I could easily imagine her being there. We went into the village church and saw the graves of Sissons (members of my mother's family) in the cemetery and called on a Mrs Minnie Sisson who, though she had lived there for sixty years, said: 'Of course, I'm Yorkshire'. She lives comfortably in a spotless cottage and with a well-tended garden. Good, country fare in a scrupulous hotel.

We then paid a call to the lady who lives in Temple Sowerby Manor: a great character, with hesitant charm, slow wit, quick eye, untidy hair, dangling earrings, tartan coat and red Russian boots, and who happens to be a cousin of the Queen Mother. A delightful visit.

On to Crossrigg Hall, belonging to a Mr Cornish Torbock — believe it or not — and his brother. Both eccentrics. The garden famous and obviously Cornish knows his various euphorbias. A Victorian house of unparalleled ugliness, a museum piece in shades of squashed strawberry and biscuit, containing not one single item of beauty to delight the eye.

We motored on through rainclouds: Borrowdale, Honister Pass, Buttermere Lake, then to Scale Hill Hotel, but too wet and clouds too low to see the promised panorama.

We made our way north. At Holyrood House we were guided by a relentless tyrant in green cap and tartan trousers. He regaled us with the impressive history of the place and stories of the Queen's entourage and her visits to the castle (many facts obviously wrong). He said that the Queen has (hideous) modern furniture brought into the rooms for her comfort. The secret staircases used by Mary Queen of Scots, Rizzio and Darnley were mysterious and thrilling; stories of court ladies forced to collect any tears they may shed in bottles to avoid marring their thickly painted complexion.

Marchmont House: *pâté de foie gras*-coloured stone, mansard roof — huge but not overbearing; wonderful plasterwork throughout — four seasons depicted in one pink room. Lady MacEwen, our hostess, was charming and remarkable — on a long refectory table in her sitting-room a huge panorama of small photographs of her family were interspersed with set pieces of flowers arranged formally. A tour of the garden — her personality impressive, her speech exquisitely precise, good jokes, intelligence, no selfishness or 'cut-off' feeling, though she is widowed and stays here all year.

While travelling we notice how pop art has made one conscious of the aesthetic effects of quite ordinary road-repairing and maintenance signs and directions — the red arrow, the discs, the cones of rubber marking the borders of danger areas, the Day-glo colours, orange and apricot, of the workmen's special jackets. High-tension wires are pure Klee or Buffet.

Then to Pitlochry, where I last went as a child. I had not seen the Highlands since then and I was thrilled.

The hotel, beautifully situated over an Altdorfer forest of trees, possessed none of its furnishings of fifty years before, and none of its powers to impress. However, it was good to savour this fresh Scottish air again, and the smell of the brooks and bracken and heather.

On to Perth Castle. This was just what we were looking for — a riot of stuffed stags' heads, antlers, weapons of aggression, guns, spears, all displayed with the tasteless meticulousness that is really an art in itself. Tartan beds, four-posters with mad ostrich feathers, Victoriana, early photographs, good and bad collections of every sort all jumbled together. The crowds were so delighted to find no guides to keep them in control that they ran in every direction, up and down polished staircases, in and out of bedrooms and bathrooms. The white pebble-dash with which the castle is covered is better than the usual cream, and the black roofs and turrets give the wild impression of Scotland that we have so far missed.

Early departure for a hell of a drive — Scottish holiday over — now down to Durham at rush-hour in time to see the cathedral and the Venerable Bede's tomb. The scale is tremendous — marvellous proportions, thick arches, decorated with the simple, crude design cut into the stone. The best cathedral in England.

To step into Bindie Lambton's world of children and dogs was quite a shock. We ate marrow bones for dinner in a room with the beautifully brought-up dogs asleep in niches, each with their brass plates on them, under the china cabinets.

Long drive on main roads, including the M1, at tremendous speed. King's Lynn for lunch at the delightful eighteenth-century hotel in the main square; delight at Norfolk Dutch atmosphere; pretty gabled houses; no Woolworths, no new building. A Festival of Constable, Henry Moore and Sybil Cholmondeley.

'Why didn't you let me know before. All I can offer you is tea at five o'clock with the Queen Mother and twelve guests from Sandringham.' In fact we welshed. We were too ragged in body and mind to make the necessary readjustment. But we did go to see Sibyl, and as we were going down the tall avenue on our way to her glorious house we were so impressed that we got out of the car and changed our trousers.

The house and its furnishings are superb. Sybil, calm and funny, well-informed and no-nonsense, showed us all.

Part II: The Chosen Ones, 1964-7

LYDIA LOPOKOVA

Thursday, July 30th 1964

An American lady wanted to rent Reddish House. Her offer was accepted and within four days we had to turn out — sad, but this was an easy way of making money and it only entailed leaving the house four days earlier than intended.

The packing up and emptying of cupboards, the tidying and scouring was an endless job. I had to fight to get some writing done and to get to Wilton for tennis.

Never has there been a lovelier summer. For weeks the weather has held. The garden flourishing pink, white and grey. The trees have become dark, almost black, and all the flowers from childhood holidays — phlox, Japanese azaleas, nasturtiums and hollyhocks — have come out, which in a way makes it a melancholy time. For it means that when we return from our holiday, the long, long awaited summer will be over; there will be a different outlook; fires will be on and there will not again be the delight of leaving doors and windows wide open.

However, our high spirits revived in the company of Lydia Lopokova, whom we visited in her farmhouse at Tilton. She is fatter, older, like a little Russian peasant and her clothes are as extraordinary as ever — Statler, Statler, Statler was printed on her apron, a twenty-year-old theft from the USA — but she has quietened a little. She did not laugh quite as much as she used to, and her gestures and pantomime were mostly done from her chair. But she gives freshness to everything and no one is less snobbish than she. She does not know the meaning of the word.

When she comes to London her treat is to go to a restaurant in the Tottenham Court Road where she orders meat spaghetti *con burro*. She showed us two piles of clothes returned from the laundry. She praised a blouse she had bought for thirty shillings from Marks and Spencer, 'and see how nicely it washes! It looks Russian!'

She describes her life: 'I like to eat dinner in the company of someone, so Maynard's adopted son comes and we eat steak. I spend my day, naked to the waist, leaning over the raspberries on the cane. It is good with the sun on my back and I eat two raspberries for every one I put in the basket. I no longer use my arms and hands like a dancer.' The hall was lined with cups, pots, pans, kitchen implements. 'I love being alone — it's so tiring to see neighbours. I love my house here. These aren't my paintings.' (Not true!) 'They belong to King's College, but I can have them for my lifetime — Cézannes, Picasso, Braque, Degas, Modigliani.'

She described her shopping expedition to buy food. 'The International Stores is wonderful, but such crowds. It's like Auschwitz. I used to pick peas but they're just as good from the deep freeze. I read the *Manchester Guardian*. I love the Beatles and went to see *Lord of the Flies*, and went to the ballet, *La Fille Mal Gardée*, at Eastbourne.'

For two hours she talked, refused to be photographed, entranced us with the *mot juste*. Kin said that of all the houses he'd seen in England he would most prefer to have hers, with its quiet, arched courtyard and simple decorations.

Went on to Eastbourne. We walked up to Beachy Head and looked down on where St Cyprian's had been. Schoolday memories flooded.

Then to dine with old St Cyprian, Cyril Connolly. He was funny about Lopokova being like Duchesse de Guermantes.

Finishing up *Diaries*, volume V — the last job before starting off on our journey abroad. One by one the phases of the summer are ticked off. The tour of Cornwall, Yorkshire, Scotland and Norfolk ... the packing up and preparations for Munich, Sienna, Venice, Turkey.

Venice: Tuesday, August 25th

I don't know what happens to me in Venice, but after a few days in the sun and beauty the atmosphere depresses me. The unconscious moments before waking are sad, and on surfacing my thoughts are morbid.

I am seldom a victim of depression, but today and yesterday too I felt I didn't really want to go on living much more. I've been very happy this summer, and maybe I'm just tired; perhaps it's being with someone thirty years younger than I am that keeps me invigorated, in touch, alert, and alive to new ideas.

But suddenly I feel old, lacking in enthusiasm. I feel my work inadequate. Seeing the great masters brings one to despair. There is no time or energy left for me to improve; the old life is outmoded and done for. What to take its place? Perhaps these feelings will leave me on returning home, but Venice has activated something that is deep down in my bones. I don't like it to come to the surface. For this reason I will be pleased to leave.

A VISIT TO TURKEY

September 1964

I had not visited Istanbul since those years before the war when Ataturk was intent on bringing Turkey out of the dark Ottoman past. Men in the dusty, old-fashioned streets then wore the tarboosh, together with an appalling mixture of Oriental and Europeanized garments: braces on jellabas; bicycle clips on pyjama trousers. Today the tarboosh is forbidden, and the whole city is unrecognizable with skyscrapers, neon lights, apartment buildings, and a Hilton Hotel, where we stayed. From the windows we could see the Bosphorus and the Sea of Marmara, a mêlée of ships, buses, motors, fishermen, scurrying pedestrians, pop-art advertisements, a world of flurry and movement, of steam and smoke belching from ships' funnels, water churning in torrents in the wake of every sort of pleasure boat and barge, clouds parting to illuminate the ancient water tower, minarets like exclamation marks, and the appetizing-looking fish, fruit, and sweet stalls.

We went across the Galata Bridge to see Santa Sophia: vast, an overwhelming effect of glowing gold and dusty decoration; an incredible dome, with four enormous, suspended shields covered with Turkish calligraphy; innumerable wrought-iron chandeliers hanging low to the ground appeared dwarfed in the huge space; in the gloom, unexpectedly, a mosaic head of Christ, some green, strange saints, huge Ali Baba pots; all very mysterious. The most beautiful of all Istanbul's religious buildings is the small jewel box of the Kariye, which is in an astonishing excellence of preservation with fine frescoes, inlaid marble panelling, and sequin-glittering mosaic of infinite refinement.

The next excitement was to visit the Seraglio — the mansion — place of the Moslem Ottoman emperors, the palace of the sultans — to see the possessions of former sultans; an extraordinary collection of unmatched luxury. There was more blue and white porcelain that I had ever seen before; Sèvres clocks under glass domes and much china. A jewel-studded ceremonial throne of thirty-six-carat gold, a pair of forty-eight-carat gold candlesticks with over six thousand diamonds in each, emeralds as big as ducks' eggs, huge pink diamonds (bright violet pink), goblets of crystal inlaid with jewels, feathers made of diamonds, a blob of emerald weighing over three kilos, and the 'spoon seller's diamond' of eighty-six-carats set in a circle of half a hundred huge diamonds. The central colonnaded gardens with rococo, wooden-carved doorways were a joy to come out into as we progressed from one pavilion to another. The costumes of the sultans on display were of boldly designed, magnificent silks, marvellous audacity of colour, reds predominant, and they undoubtedly inspired Bakst and the Diaghilev ballet.

The Turkish landscape is dry, hot, and often of bare rock and hard desert, but it also offers a variety of lush plains, feathery forests, purple mountains and scented groves. It took me several days to realize that the sweetness so often in the air came from the fig trees. White cattle draw huge cartloads, people pick cotton in the fields, and there are camels — beautiful, touching, proud and ridiculous.

High along the Bosphorus and among the clouds rises the invulnerable fortress of the Rumeli Lisar Castle, with its crenellated towers, a medieval castle *par excellence*. On a massive scale, it is the perfect realization of the cardboard, cut-out castles we played with as children. Today it is inhabited only by crows, and deserted except for an occasional production of *Coriolanus*.

A trip by boat to one of the four neighbouring islands is the means whereby many Istanbulis escape the heat of summer. Boyokada, the favourite resort of the rich, has a pervasive pre-1914 war, or strangely timeless, feeling. Many of the houses, with their elaborately carved wooden facades, are reminiscent of those in the lazy southern states of America. This unreal, in-a-dream atmosphere is emphasized by the fact that no motor cars are allowed, and the castanet click of hooves is continuous as the population travel in fringe-covered wicker-basket carriages. In spite of the busy army of street cleaners, the scent of the pinewoods is mingled with the equally pungent aroma of fresh horse-dung. The smell of thyme or curry-like herbs is usually in one's nostrils; even the smallest window is scented with basil, honeysuckle or jasmine.

Izmir (the ancient Smyrna of fig fame) is now a pulsating, ever-growing modern town, with clusters of skyscrapers and minarets piercing the skyline. In the pleasure gardens the Industrial Fair offered, in the pavilions of all countries, the latest in scientific inventions; a contrast to ancient works of art in the archaeological museum. The modern market, alas, did not please us; very little was locally made and all that one could buy were plastic gadgets, hideous, vulgar and impersonal.

To me, many of the temples, agoras and broken theatres in Turkey are merely a picturesque shambles: the splinters and fragments of former greatness have a certain monotony. But the remains of Ephesus are different; it is its scale that impresses; marble roads, flanked with marble and stone buildings, stretching by the mile up the mountainside. Built in honour of Artemis in the eleventh century, it has been occupied by Lydians, Persians, Syrians, Romans and Byzantines, who have all left their mark. The entrance to the Temple of Hadrian is beautiful. The small Odeon, a theatre for chamber orchestra and intimate plays, delighted me more than the almost staggeringly large theatre nearby with seating capacity for nearly twenty-five thousand people.

Priene lies above the curling Meander River (from which the word is derived) on a huge promontory like the prow of a ship. It is a masterpiece of town planning, with its buildings placed in grid design, and gives, as in San Francisco, vistas of great splendour at the end of each street. Here avid archaeologists wander among the relics of the gymnasiums, temples, and senate.

1965

Alan Tagg used to be so timid that it was impossible to hear his whispers hidden behind a curtain of fair hair. Now he has blossomed, and when given a sympathetic audience he can be devastatingly funny for long leisurely spans of time.

He has been beguiling us with anecdotes of his recent visit to America and each story is told with such exactitude of dialogue, and is in itself so carefully chosen and individual, that one gets the very essence of his experiences. Likewise, when he described his ecstasy of amusement at the play *Sin*, and described the evening's entertainment, we might all have been present at the performance.

A delightful aspect of Alan's humour is that once something has struck him as funny, it is always funny and can be enjoyed over and over again with pristine relish. Suddenly he will explode with mirth and in explanation tell us that he has just remembered something he heard one woman say to another in a bus ten years ago. 'What was it, do let us share the joke?' 'Well, one woman said, "I washed it for her when she was eighteen, I washed it for her when she was twenty-one, I washed it for her when she was married, and I washed it after her first-born, but I'm never going to wash it for her again."'

We were talking of John Gielgud who had directed a little family comedy for which Alan had done the décor. John has always been tactless, and has developed the art of saying exactly what is on his mind to the most farcical extent. In his deep, throaty, almost military, staccato voice he keeps up a flow without ever noticing the reaction it may have on others. At one rehearsal he says: 'You're beginning to be very good. I'm *very* pleased with you all, except, of course, Berty — you've got it all wrong — no good at all.' Berty explodes into noisy tears. John, stricken with embarrassment and avoiding a row at all costs, is not seen for dust.

One poor girl does not see that a piece of scenery has been placed in her way, falls over it with a painful thud. 'Oh, Dilys, do be graceful!' remarks John.

Alan decries himself, surprised when directors pay him a compliment. 'They seem to like my work! Of course I'd like to do something with a modern author. But they send me things I don't understand. This new Joe Orton play, for example, all the cast say the most awful things to one another!'

DAVID HOCKNEY

As a child I was, like most Edwardians, brought up never to waste a mouthful of food. 'If you can't finish your lunch, you'll have it cold for supper. Waste not, want not,' was drummed in and somehow my father always instilled into us a fear of the workhouse.

How very different the youth of today. David Hockney arrived (to be painted) on his way from Bristol. He turned up in his car wearing the thinnest of synthetic windbreakers over a T-shirt. 'Noh, I'm nut corld. Is it corld outside? I get into my car and the heat's automatically on and I get out at the plaice I arrive at. You may think this cappe is a bit daft, but I bought ert at Arrods because I wasn't looking whaire I was gohin and I knocked over all the hat stall and I put the mun to so mooch trooble, I thought ah moost buy sommut!'

Likewise, nothing seems to surprise him. A boy from a humble family in the Midlands, he arrived to learn to be a 'paintah' in London without any misgivings. 'It was most extraordinary at the college. After a bit they wouldn't give me any more cunvass, or paints, because I hadn't got any munnay, so that's how I got interested in engraving. They let you have the stoof free, but even so they said I was waaistin their copper plates because I did static isolated line drawings of figures they said I should use up all the copper by covering it with pattern. Before someone came and gave me a prize (for that picture you bought), they never thought anything of my work. Now I paint twenty pictures a year and Kas[5] sells the lot; and I teach. I luv America and I teach there quite a lot. They can't paint a sphere, so I set the class to paint a door. They all got canvases the size of a door and painted as realistically as possible and we had an exhibition of all the doors down a corridor. It looked naice. But I couldn't get oop in the momins. I was supposed to start at eight-thairtee, but I'd paaint at night and then go out to the poobs until they closed and that'd be two o'clock, and perhaps it was three or four before I got to baid, so I couldn't get up at eight o'clock, so I'd go in at ten-thirty and stay till one, but no one seemed to caire.'

[5] Kasmin, David Hockney's dealer.

It staggers me how this young man can be so at home in the world. When *I* first went to America, I was too scared to ask a policeman which was up or down town. Not David! He arrives in Los Angeles without knowing a soul. He gets arrested at three in the morning for jay-walking; he makes a lot of friends and goes off in a truck with one to try and get a driving licence. 'Where's your car?' 'I haven't got one, but this is my friend's trook.' He drives it around with the instructor, who thinks him mad — quite understandably because David had never driven before — but who nevertheless gives him his licence. Hockney then buys a car and starts to drive it on the St Bernadino freeway. He can't get off it, so has to drive on and on until he comes, four hours later, to Las Vegas. He stays there for an hour then comes all the way back. 'It gives you confidence to be driving for ten hours on end.'

PHOTOGRAPHING PICASSO

April 28th, 1965

It is strange that, at my age, I should work myself up into such a nervous condition at the idea of photographing Picasso. I was certainly extremely on edge, I remember, when I first photographed him in the Rue de la Boetie in the early thirties. At that time I could speak very little French. In the meantime every photographer in the world, and thousands of amateurs too, have had a field day with him; I remember Alexander Liberman saying it was tiresome that once one had photographed Picasso, he had never had enough and begged one to come back tomorrow.

I sent a telegram as from le Petit Beaton from London to warn him of my arrival. I was in a state of anticipation by the time I arrived at the Grand Hotel, Cannes. Five minutes later I was on my way in a taxi to the Notre Dame de Vie at Mougins.

I realized what a tremendous number of canvases must have been sold to pay for this long, winding drive that circled to the top of the mountain. Suddenly a closed gate, with a bell. The driver rang. No answer. I would not have been surprised if they had not answered. It could have been like the end of *Washington Square*. But, suddenly a voice asked who was there. 'Mr Beaton? Mr Cecil Beaton?' 'Yes.' 'Then wait.' The door eventually opened and we were suddenly in a courtyard filled with brilliant mauve wisteria and being welcomed by Madame Picasso.

Madame Picasso is squat and short-necked. She wore a blue silk coat and white trousers, hair immaculate. She was very polite. 'Pablo says it is twenty years since he last saw you. Please come in.'

A great welcome from Picasso. 'Oh, I am *pleased* that you are here. We must embrace.' I kissed him on two, soft, cleanly shaven cheeks.

Also present were Monsieur and Madame Gomez (she specializes in the works of Balthus) and the room was a kaleidoscope of brilliant objects and colours against a sunny white background.

Picasso, sad to relate, had aged and it had taken the form of shrivelling him. There was something melancholy about his eyes, which had lost some of their brilliance; before they were black, but now they seemed a light brown. His skin was pale cigar-leaf and his hands and pointed fingers, rather heavy, were a darker shade; the teeth like old ivory and the whites of the eyes parchment. In fact, in his several sweaters and velvet trousers, he was altogether a symphony of brown, beige and mushroom. There was a gash of green paint on one arm and a sleeve was worn to tatters, a hole also in the black stockings; neat white leather shoes.

Lots of fun about the passage of the years. Yes, he remembered my photographing him like Whistler's mother and featuring the toys on his mantelpiece. No regrets about the dead or the past. We must go on even if it was madness. The numbers of paintings he did! Sometimes eight in one day. We must see everything there is to see. 'Come!'

We left his sitting-room for another white, simple drawing-room with such a mass of letters, pottery, drawings and stacks of canvas that it was impossible to take in more than an occasional detail. Past the dark dining-room with the long table covered with parcels, pictures, books, sculpture, and pictures stacked against the wall, to the hall, full of packing cases and canvases. Down to the basement (formerly the hall in the Guinness' time), now just a cemetery of modern statuary, some lifelike, others abstract constructions of wire, steel, painted tin. Picasso wandered about turning on extra lights for the photographs; he enjoyed being taken, was amused and flattered; he had a semi-queasy expression on his face. He gazed at the camera with wildly staring eyes, and I took a lot of pictures as we continued our tour of the house.

The amount of work by Picasso was utterly staggering. But there was more. 'Come you must see everything. This is nothing.' Madame Picasso was self-effacing and managed to be out of the camera line all the time, and when I did try to take her, she seemed genuinely unhappy and shy. We then climbed a white circular staircase to one huge painting-room after another. Each was filled with pictures, some not finished and still wet, everywhere large daubs of the shapes we have become accustomed to; but to me the latest work seemed to have lost exactitude. The line was not good; the brush stroke coarse and rubbed. A lot of curious painting with every sort of trick employed; sometimes he dipped a cork into the paint and pressed that on to the canvas; a smell of Ripolin and everywhere stacks of tins of paint. Even on a huge glassed-in terrace, with a superb view of distant purple mountains, there were masses of blue canvases, mostly of monstrous women, all somewhat indecent according to Victorian standards.

The sun poured through the shutters which, because of the high wind, slashed backwards and forwards. I clicked and clicked, hoping for the best in my excitement; I moved a piece of sculpture that I thought was made of card and found it was of iron; points dug into my thumb and the blood poured. Nothing to do but suck and forget. Some of the time the sun came through onto the floor and enabled me to take good patterned compositions, but much of the 'work' was pretty humdrum stuff and God knows if I got the exposures right.

Back in the first sitting-room we sat around the circular table and talked happily. In the centre of the table there was a bowl of deep-pink roses from the garden, and around the room in odd pots delightful little posies of daisies, tulips and small, bright, wild flowers. I went on taking pictures.

When I felt I had taken enough I got out my sketch book; but I found that after the intensity of taking photographs my energies were too dissipated for drawing. I kept turning the pages. Picasso rushed from his chair. 'You do what Degas did and have pages that are transparent, so that you can turn over and trace the good bits and ignore the bad.' He was tremendously enthusiastic about this idea and his eyes popped. It was another facet of his extraordinary display of vitality.

At one point he demonstrated to M. Gomez the advantages of the modern (Knoll) swivel chair he sat in. He almost twirled himself into space. All his actions were quick ones; his arms raised in a jerk; his body too nervous and tense to be graceful. Generally when he turned his head, his body turned too. He jumped from place to place like a boy skipping. He talked of his working at night. Then it was quiet, with no one to disturb him. Sometimes it was three o'clock before he stopped, so he got up late in the morning. He didn't need much sleep but liked to rest and read. When someone complained that they hadn't been able to sleep, Picasso said: 'So much the better for you. Sleep is a waste.' He is strong; he is accustomed to moving sculpture. He did an imitation of his mother in her working chair. Her feet could never touch the ground. He asked Madame Gomez why she was here. 'Specially to see you.' That reminded me that Alice Toklas arrived one day and said she had come especially to see him. 'Now you've seen me, you can go.' Alice was not amused. But Picasso is fond of Alice and is still helping her through the financial difficulties she was in after the death of her friend Stein. Picasso sometimes stared very intently at me and his regard still has the power to intimidate. He laughed at me holding four sharpened pencils in my hand and said: 'Aren't you going to paint me?' He said he thought I *was* a painter. I had the eyes of a painter, like Chardin or Fragonard, but not of a photographer. Most photographers had eyes like lenses. Photographs were too mechanical. Drawings were more alive, and colour photographs added nothing to black and white.

Madame Gomez went into the next room to talk business with Picasso, and Madame Picasso told me that she still found Pablo someone that she could never take for granted. She had been married for eleven years and each day was more impressed by his honesty and naturalness. He was so great that she felt it was a privilege to be with him and take care of him. It is clear how much she loves him. Her eyes linger on him.

She dashes forward in distress if, the wind blowing one canvas on to another, they have smudged. She wraps his jumper across his chest when he comes out into the open. She brings him a large glass of milk.

Jacqueline Picasso admitted she would like to go to Paris; that they seldom went out here, not even to the bull fights any more. Pablo only liked to work; his world was here on the mountain top. He had already made three new studios and he wants to fill a fourth. This at eighty-four is not bad! She is obviously perfectly happy to look after this man and has no ulterior motives.

Time to go. 'I have to paint,' said the master. It is marvellous that he has such gaiety at his time of life.

I had been somewhat suffocated by too many neo-classical heads and tortured buttocks and graffiti-esque twats; and there were too many photographs of Picasso around. But he had been kindness itself to me.

'So good to see you looking so well,' I said and he ran to touch wood. He does not like the process of getting old. 'Come back again in twenty years, but come back sooner as well.' Eyes melting with amusement and friendliness, he waved as we circled down the mountainside.

July 1965

For many, many years Juliet Duff has been a great figure in my life, and has had a certain influence on me. Her taste, inherited from her mother,[6] has always impressed me, and she has an elegance and a sense of eccentricity that is appealing. But I have never really liked her, nor she me.

---

[6] Lady Ripon (daughter of Lord Herbert of Lea, the Victorian politician).

At first she was very undecided as to whether she would 'take me up' or not. At the time of my 'first appearance' in London she was an intimate friend of Diaghilev, sitting in his box at the first night of the new ballet season. It was to a large supper-party in her Belgrave Square house that she first invited me. The fifty guests were already seated at a long table in the dining-room; marble swans looked on. Everyone was drinking pink champagne, a drink always served by her mother. Most of the men guests were in dinner jackets. I, arriving late, had to walk the length of the room to greet my hostess. I was in a tail coat, having come on from some other beano that warranted such apparel. Emerald Cunard on seeing me created a little rumpus of displeasure, for only a few days before she had thrown on to the fire and put a poker through my recently published *Book of Beauty* declaring that I was a 'low fellow'. Juliet was now in a quandary. As hostess she must be polite to her *invité*, but although she never liked Emerald she did not necessarily want to incur her wrath. With one gracious smile I was bidden to sit out of earshot and sight of Emerald, and from that day on Juliet has been a constant friend.

As the years pass, Juliet's once enormous income has diminished; she has had to retrench, and her innate meanness has taken a severe hold. The slate mines have been doing badly in Wales, so she must sell a Fabergé ornament or a Boilly painting.

Sunday

Today, however, Juliet was at her best; she sat back and listened to the talk, which was racy. Occasionally she made a contribution about someone she considered eccentric and interesting. Simon, rather tipsy, was in his most delightful vein and at the end of the evening he ran his hand down Juliet's arm and said: 'You've looked so pretty in your rose-coloured dress.'

But lately we have become alarmed, for Juliet's health is very poor. She has fallen several times and although Dr Gottfried has reduced her blood pressure from the danger point, she does not look as if she will be long in this world. Then one day she keeled over getting out of bed. The doctor was called and she was ordered to rest. The next day she had a brain haemorrhage, lost consciousness, and died.

Although in many ways Juliet and I did not get on, I know I shall miss her.

Kin's exit was as if to an execution. In my pyjamas I watched him go. He had two heavy bags to carry. He gripped his lips tightly and looked very serious. I like to think that it was as bad a moment for him as it was for me. The taxi came. His outstretched hand was stiff and taut. I went back to bed, not to sleep, but to moan at my loss and to feel desperately sad.

GRETA IN GREECE

July 1965

I arrived at Vouliagmeni, the appointed bay where the yachts were harboured. Greta was the first person I saw; sitting with her back to the quay she had tied her hair back with a rubber band into a small pigtail. The effect was pleasing, neat and Chinese, but the hair has become grey. The surprised profile turned to reveal a big smile.

She was up to her old tricks. 'My, my, my! Can it be Beattie, my Beat!' Still feeling Kin's presence, I took the opportunity to tell her of his leaving this morning after one year. 'One whole year! My, my!' was all she had to say on the subject. There are so many things that we could have shared. At first I was riled and irritated by the 'Is that so's' and 'never mind's', 'Don't ask questions', 'Not going to tell you', etc. I couldn't imagine that there was not to be one moment of truth; but, no, she behaved like a mad child most of the time and that is all she wanted. So I soon learnt to talk gibberish like a monkey and she seemed perfectly content.

Greta's sense of humour is very alive. She remembers things that have amused her years before, including silly stories; bald man going into drug store: 'Are you sure this hair restorer will be a success? Yes? Then give me two bottles and a comb and brush.' The pansy who was told by the director to walk down the stairs in a more manly fashion: 'You don't expect me to play a character part for £7 a day?'

In the apricot-coloured light of evening she still looks absolutely marvellous; she could be cleverly photographed to appear as beautiful as ever in films, but it is not just her beauty that is dazzling; it is the mysteriousness and other intangible qualities that make her appealing, particularly when talking with sympathy and wonder to children, or reacting herself to some situation with all the innocence and surprise of childhood itself.

Tricheni

Yesterday was a halcyon day in all respects. We arrived at a sandy, olive-planted island called Tricheni that appeared to be deserted; the captain warned us of the danger of sharks. Some bathed close to the shore in pellucid waters. It was difficult to imagine anything as violent as sharks in these calm waters, but Frederick Ledebur, having demonstrated at breakfast how to baffle a wasp (by twirling one's thumb in quick circles), gave us the drill if we met a shark — splash the surface of the water and make a loud noise causing bubbles to rise. If the shark is not then terrified, dive at it; in no event turn your back on it and swim away.

While we bathed, Greta went for a walk among the olive trees; and was seen moving at a great speed in her tall straw hat, having abandoned the top to her bathing suit. A while later she returned radiant, her eyes blazing, teeth showing in a great grin. 'You have no idea how beautiful it is! It's Holy!' For the rest of the day her spirits soared. She was reborn.

By degrees we made friends with villagers, and old women bowed from their cloistered arches with the dignity of Proustian duchesses. We discovered that part of the cloisters had been converted into a *pension*, the bedrooms simple yet all that the soul requires, the dining-room appetizing. The light became more beautiful, our mood more idyllic, and we lingered, determined to come back to this place. A village girl came up to know if Greta was who she was; Greta hid her smiling face. Then as we moved on, she went back and told the girl that indeed she was who she was. The girl was delighted. Greta showed in many ways that she can be kind and good and adorable.

She talked about the Kabuki actors and said that at first she found the noises they made offensive; but on a second visit she was fascinated; and she was able to reproduce the sounds exactly. She described a female impersonator in the troupe whom she said had the most 'sexy' look of any woman she had ever seen.

Greta gave a brilliant, glowing performance as a character in a Comédie Française love drama. Her few words of French were used to miraculous effect and she was inspired and made us roar with laughter as she yearned towards the plump, honest and true little Jeanne Marie de Broglie, saying, '*ma souffrance me mange*'. The crew too were fascinated by her clowning and the captain exploded into paroxysms of mirth at her imitations of his radio talks to Athens. It is remarkable that at sixty she still possesses qualities of beauty and naturalness to such a degree.

The Studio at Reddish House: 1965

My discoveries in painting continue throughout the long hours. Apart from the technical problems of keeping a consistency of paint or brush stroke, of doing only what the medium can tolerate, other ineffable problems arise; for example where emphasis should lie, what colours do to one another, how to achieve calm or brilliance, etc. But at the moment my greatest difficulty, and one that I have really only overcome in the John Russell picture, is how to simplify right down to the essentials. This cannot be done at a late stage by adjustments with paint, brush or rag; the amount of work to be done on the picture must be in the mind's eye at the outset. At the moment I am trying hard to learn that the less one puts on to the canvas, the more successful the result is likely to be, and yet this does not always work.

Venice: August 18th

Yesterday evening a little expedition was made to visit the grave of Diaghilev on the anniversary of his death. It is the nicest thing about Serge Lifar that he comes to Venice each August 18th for this purpose, and he was childish and happy and enthusiastic that Diana Cooper and 'the boys' should come with him to pay homage.

I arrived at the cemetery before the others, got a key from a custodian and went into the green garden of the Greek Orthodox cemetery where Diaghilev lay. It was a pretty, calm, peaceful garden of motionless cypresses and a somewhat untidy tangle of shrubs and roses. Diaghilev's tomb, under a small tree, a domed ceiling above a severe slab of stone with a circle, a cross, an inscription and the name, was a suitable resting place for a great man, exiled from his native land.

I remembered how much he had meant to me in my formative years. It was a lonely sight. Diana in a large picture hat was carrying over her shoulder huge branches of bay leaves. She was dressed in her typical *café-crème*, and in the kind soft light of evening she looked as she did thirty years ago. She was followed by Lifar and by Simon Fleet looking Edwardian in Henley-on-Thames straw boater. Someone had suggested bringing Diaghilev's beloved tuberoses, but Diana said 'No, tuberoses for a virgin, bay for a man.' Diana threw down her armful with a ferocious gesture; the emotion that inspired her to make this expedition was covered by a bluff jollity. Simon and the boys took a snapshot and, after we had walked about a bit and seen where Gabriel Wolkov was recently laid to rest near his relations, we went back to the water's edge by the church.

London: September 10th
What a very different opinion Balanchine holds on Pavlova. He told me he thought she was awful. 'She had bad taste and chose dreadful music. She liked Hungarian composers and dainty, tippety-tip dances. Ta, Ta, Ta, Ta, Ta, Ta; Dimty, Dimty, Dimty — Turn! And her feet were ugly, such large, lumpy shoes. And her dresses! She'd dress up as a *marquise* with a beauty spot and do the gavotte. It was terrible, but the

audiences loved it. They didn't know any better in those days. They loved the dying swan, just for one reason, there are only about two movements in it and the hands go flap, flap, but the audience know she's going to die, so they're all waiting for it to happen. But she wasn't an artist. She didn't get along with Diaghilev; she was selfish. Yes, I knew her. She wasn't interesting. She didn't inspire men.'

I have worked with George Balanchine (on *Swan Lake*), but have never felt anything but his coldness and my own inadequacy. Tonight he was at ease and so was I. We talked of the genius of Karinska, of my thrill at the beautiful costumes she has created with my designs for *Traviata*. George said there is no one like her. 'When she is gone it will be finished and the same with me and with you too. We will not survive another twenty years, but then something quite different will happen. It will never be the same.'

He told me that nowadays he had to be careful what projects he undertook. 'You see, I can only teach people by showing them myself how it must be done and it is terribly tiring. I can't do all this jumping and dancing much longer, and so I must not take on something that will take me four months to prepare, unless it is really worth it; it's not worth it in opera. I like singers to stand still, but it is much harder to get them to do it than to make dancers dance. Nureyev came to see me shortly after he fled from Russia, but he wanted to dance "on circuit" and make extra money. He wanted to be the star. He didn't want to be part of a ballet. He is too selfish and a dancer cannot afford to be selfish. You will soon spot a selfish dancer. Nureyev will end up badly, you'll see. He'll be like Pavlova.'

New York: November 10th

Five o'clock: the fitting of our 'Violetta' in her Karinska costumes was over. Everyone pleased.

People in the streets hurrying like black ants, trying in vain to cross the road; motor cars incapable of moving. I managed to get back to my hotel to continue my work. We tried to telephone to find out what had happened, but there were no lines. There had been a complete power cut which covered the whole eastern side of the country. The revelation came slowly that not only were many people likely to be trapped in elevators and subways, but others would be marooned away from friends and families, and food in frigidaires and deep freezes would thaw. Radio and television were out of commission; hundreds of cities, towns, and villages were plunged into immobility. The boys decided to go down the staircase. A woman in the next suite came out in terror. She lent them a candle for the descent. Impotent and isolated, I returned to my room, sank on to my bed and mercifully slept.

April 11th, 1966

So Evelyn Waugh is in his coffin. Died of snobbery. Did not wish to be considered a man of letters; it did not satisfy him to be thought a master of English prose. He wanted to be a duke, and that he could never be; hence a life of disappointment and sham. For he would never give up. He would drink brandy and port and keep a full cellar. He was not a gourmet, like Cyril Connolly, but insisted on good living and cigars as being typical of the aristocratic way of life. He became pompous at twenty and developed his pomposity to the point of having a huge stomach and an ear trumpet at forty-five.

Now that he is dead, I cannot hate him; cannot really feel he was wicked, in spite of his cruelty, his bullying, his caddishness.

From time to time, having appeared rather chummy and appreciative and even funny (though my hackles rose in his presence), he would suddenly seem to be possessed by a devil and do thoroughly fiendish things. His arrogance was at its worst at White's. Here he impersonated an aristocrat, intimidated newcomers and non-members, and was altogether intolerable. But a few loyal friends saw through the pretence and were fond of him.

KARSAVINA

April 26th, 1966

An ugly little old lady turned out to be Karsavina. It must be ten years since I've seen her. She is now eighty-three. The havoc on her face made her unrecognizable. The circles under her eyes have become like porridge spilling way below her cheek bones, and she had in desperation painted a huge pale-red mouth over her own neat little lips.

However, watching her during the meal and across the large circular table (the Kenneth Clarks had invited twelve to a private room at the Ritz), one could still see by her manner that she had been beautiful. With hooded lids and the proud bearing of her head, she was obviously someone who had been much worshipped. As my neighbour, a young woman, remarked, 'They don't make them like that any more.'

Later I had a word or two with Madame Karsavina. She bemoaned the fact that she had seen the new moon through glass, so nothing had gone well. The iron gate had come off its hinges, the bath water did not function, a windowpane had been broken, the roof had leaked and a ceiling was ruined; the list went on. As she bade me kiss her goodbye, she asked me earnestly: 'Do you still think I am photogenic?'

November 27th, 1966

I have become more and more hunched and conscious of my age. One does not know what one would feel like at eighty, but the present signs are that I would prefer to snuff out pretty soon, rather than continue in the vein of the present. Apart from a painful spine, other factors have caused this depression. I am going through all my photographic files for a book that is to be called 'The Best of Beaton'. So many thousands of forgotten negatives, mostly bad, cause me to consider why I should add to their number with such effort of body and spirit. So few of them have a life of their own; so many of the subjects are no longer of interest.

What has all this been about? Merely to earn a living? If so, luckily I did not realize it at the time. To occupy the days? As I bend down to the pile of photographs on the floor, afraid of a twinge in the small of my back, I wonder if it is worthwhile ploughing through so many that have not the slightest possibility of inclusion in the book.

Suicides should take a trip before embarking upon their irrevocable decision. An hour's flight in an aeroplane and arrival in a foreign country can break the tension, or interrupt lugubrious thoughts that could lead to a willingness to drift away or a weakening of the wish to carry on the ever more exhausting fight.

Reddish: January 1967

After six months of *pourparlers*, a lorry drove up with a lot of ancient stones. These are the beginning of our new plans for the garden. We will pave over some of the flower-beds and have fewer bedded-out plants.

The trees for 'Little Japan' arrive next (the prunus and flowering fruits that are to dot the hill opposite my bedroom). We are planning for posterity. It is an act of faith, and I wish it had been done before.

The only thing that prevents my making other major alterations is money. I never know my financial situation. Eileen is in charge. I rely on her to warn me when we have spent too much. I'd like very much to improve the guest rooms, and give each its own bathroom. But Eileen says we must not do this for another two or three years. How she knows this I do not know. But here's hoping there will be no cataclysm! One can be poor when young, but never later on in life.

Part III: The Younger Generation, 1967

TUTANKHAMUN EXHIBITION

Paris

This week there were several magnets to draw me to Paris: a Turkish Princess (to be photographed), Chanel (to be half-listened to), and the Tutankhamun exhibition to see. The latter proved the most difficult. Although I got out of the hotel early in order to be at the Petit Palais before the gates opened, I discovered that five hundred people had already arrived. Perhaps when the large queue had been accommodated, I could return. But no, half an hour later the queue was longer than ever, and so it remained whenever I happened to pass throughout the day. Even at lunchtime the slow crocodile had advanced only imperceptibly.

However, on the Wednesday evening at 9.30 when Lilia Ralli and I drove past on the way to a late dinner, I saw the doors were still open and with no one entering. Then Lilia remembered there was a late showing on a Wednesday. Thus I was able to see one of the most moving exhibitions of my lifetime.

I don't know why the shock was so great. Perhaps it was that, without preparation or expectation, I was suddenly confronted with these extraordinary objects. Perhaps it was the fact that they had been brought from Cairo to Paris, and exhibited in a most dramatic way, with extraordinary lighting, that made this strong impact.

Perhaps, too, the fact that they were utterly remote, of an age of over three thousand years ago, and yet fresh and modern, made the delight acutely surprising. I know little of Egyptian art, and had seen none of these treasures when I was in Egypt during the war. But the brightness, the craftmanship, the subtlety and sophistication, struck me as sensational and yet in some way not unlike the contemporary idiom.

That they have been discovered in my lifetime, by these curious and worthy Englishmen, makes them even more romantic and important. One of the greatest moments in modern history must have been when Howard Carter, peering into the darkness of the tomb from the recently dug hole in the wall, said: 'I see wonderful things, wonderful gold things, and more than you can believe possible.'

Lilia Ralli was an excellent cicerone. She had only two days before been round the exhibition privately with Princess Marina, when they had had the services of one of the very top Egyptologists as guide.

With only half an hour on hand, we could not dawdle, and even now there was a queue to see the jewellery, but from the moment of seeing the huge carving of a head — a fragment from Karnak — high up, beautifully lit, I was as if under a spell.

Lilia pointed out the canework of the seat on the young boy-king's throne. It was still as firm as when made and could be sat on today. The painting palette of the king's sister (Princess Meritaton) was an extraordinary souvenir; the small statuettes in wood, and the alabaster figures of animals and birds, had a timeless quality.

In a low, dark room we discovered the king's bed, fortified by sacred cows of gold — (*lit véhicule évoquant la vache primordiale*) their bodies dotted with emerald spots and their tails curling like great musical instruments. The golden death-mask of the king is one of the great marvels of craftsmanship of all time.

When faced by the wonderful great stone heads, so serene and calm and time-conquering, my emotion was so great that I suddenly found myself in tears. The emotion relayed from the other visitors may also have had to do with this overwhelming effect. For the objects themselves were not only extraordinary, but they became the more so by the crowds that peered at them with such awe. This scene should have been photographed, for seldom have I seen French crowds so completely taken out of themselves, lost in the tomb of time. Their eyes were wild, their fingers frenetic. Two young lovers, very beatnik, were contorted with their arms and hands interlocked — a sort of unconscious Laocoon.

Often I am critical of myself for being so thick-skinned and immune to emotion, particularly at seeing works of art, but this occasion had been an exception. The experience of the Tutankhamun exhibition had been one of enchantment and enlightenment. For a short while I had been transported out of my normal existence by the sight of great beauty.

A gentleman of quiet Spanish pride and dignity, Balenciaga makes few pronouncements. Therefore it is of special interest when he says there are no elegant women in Paris today.

He explains that he is carrying on doing something that is nothing more nor less than a luxury. It is work with materials, needle and thread. It is not streamlined; it is not efficient. It is completely against the tide of the times we are living in.

AN EVENING WITH THE 'STONES'

Marrakesh: March 1967

On the Tuesday evening I came down to dinner very late, and, to my surprise, sitting in the hotel lobby, discovered Mick

Jagger and a sleepy looking band of gipsies. Robert Fraser, one of their company, wearing a huge, black felt hat and a bright emerald brocade coat was coughing by the swimming pool. He had swallowed something the wrong way. He recovered and invited me to join them all for a drink.

It was a strange group. The three 'Stones': Brian Jones, with his girlfriend, beatnik-dressed Anita Pallenberg — dirty white face, dirty blackened eyes, dirty canary drops of hair, barbaric jewellery — Keith Richards in eighteenth-century suit, long black velvet coat and the tightest pants; and, of course, Mick Jagger, together with hangers-on, chauffeurs, and Americans.

I didn't want to give the impression that I was only interested in Mick, but it happened that we sat next to one another as he drank a Vodka Collins and smoked with pointed finger held high. His skin is chicken-breast white and of a fine quality. He has an inborn elegance. He talked of native music; he had heard a local tribe play pipes like those used in Hungary and Scotland. He liked Indian music too. He said he would like to go to Kashmir and to Afghanistan, in fact to get right away from England, which he considered had become a police state, with harassment and interference. Recently twenty policemen had invaded the house of his drummer in the country looking for dope. The newspapers had published completely false accounts. He was going to sue the *News of the World*. He maintained that he had done nothing to deprave the youth of the country. Here in Morocco people were not curious or bad-mannered. He liked people that were permissive.

By degrees the shy aloofness of the gang broke down. We got into two cars; the Bentley I was in had been driven from Brian Jones's house in Swiss Cottage to here, and the driver was a bit tired. The car was filled with pop-art cushions, scarlet fur rugs, and sex magazines. Immediately the most tremendous volume of pop music boomed in the region of the back of my neck. Mick and Brian responded rhythmically and the girl leant forward and screamed in whispers that she had just played a murderess in a film that was to be shown at the Cannes Festival.

We went to a Moroccan restaurant — tiles, banquettes, women dancers. Mick considered the style of decoration gave little opportunity of expression to the artist. He is very gentle, and with perfect manners. He indicated that I should follow his example and eat the chicken in my fingers. It was tender and good. He has much appreciation, and his small, albino-fringed eyes notice everything. 'How different and more real this place is to Tangier — the women more rustic, heavy, lumpy, but their music very Spanish and their dancing too.' He has an analytical slant and compares everything he is seeing here with earlier impressions in other countries.

Mick liked the new ballet *Paradise Lost*, but was bored by Stravinsky's *Les Noces*. He is limited in his field of music to what he had studied since he was eleven years old and which is the kind of music he plays now.

'What marvellous authority she has,' he said, listening to a coloured singer. 'She follows through.' He sent his arms jerking about him. I was fascinated with the thin concave lines of his body, legs and arms. The mouth is almost too large; he is beautiful and ugly, feminine and masculine: a rare phenomenon.

I was not disappointed and as the evening wore on found him easier to talk with. He asked: 'Have you ever taken LSD? Oh, I should. It would mean so much to you; you'd never forget the colours. For a painter it is a great experience. One's brain works not on four cylinders but on four thousand. You see everything aglow. You see yourself beautiful and ugly, and other people as if for the first time. Oh yes, you should take it in the country, surrounded by all those flowers. You'd have no bad effects. It's only people who hate themselves who suffer.' He had great assurance. 'If you enjoyed the bhang in India, this is a thousand times better: so much stronger — good stuff. Oh no, they can't stamp it out. It's like the atom bomb. Once it's been discovered, it can never be forgotten, and it's too easy to make.'

We walked through the deserted, midnight streets. Mick admired the Giacometti-like doorways; was sad at the sleeping bundles of humanity, and had not seen such poverty since Singapore. He loved the old town with its mysterious alleyways.

By the time we reached the hotel it was three o'clock and my bedtime, but they were quite happy to go on. Never a yawn and they had been up since five o'clock this morning.

It is a way of life very different from mine and I enjoyed being jerked out of myself. Mick listened to pop records for a couple of hours, and was then so tired that he went to sleep without taking off his clothes. He woke at eight, undressed and got into bed to sleep for another couple of hours.

At eleven o'clock he appeared at the swimming pool. I could not believe it was the same person walking towards us. The very strong sun, reflected from the white ground, made his face look a white, podgy, shapeless mess; eyes very small, nose very pink and spreading, hair sandy dark. His figure, his hands and arms were incredibly feminine.

None of them was willing to talk except in spasms. No one could make up their minds what to do, or when.

I took Mick through the trees to an open space to photograph him in the midday sun. I gave his face the shadows it needed. The lips were of a fantastic roundness, the body

almost hairless, and yet, surprisingly, I made him look like a
Tarzan by Pietro da Cosimo. He is sexy, yet completely sexless.
He could nearly be an eunuch. As a model he is a natural.

Their wardrobe is extensive. Mick showed me the rows of
brocade coats. Everything is shoddy, poorly made, the seams
burst. Keith himself had sewn his trousers, lavender and dull
rose, with a band of badly stitched leather dividing the two
colours.

Brian, at the pool, appears in white pants with a huge black
square applied on to the back. It is very smart, in spite of the
fact that the seams are giving way. But with such marvellously
flat, tight, compact figures as they have, with no buttocks or
stomach, almost anything looks well on them.

Marrakesh to Tangier

Beautiful roads through hills to Essaouira. In rocky hills an old
woman with orange scarf was throwing stones to move on her
flocks of goats which were eating the berries in the argan trees.
Goats in trees a strange sight. Deserted forts, markets, mud
villages. Our conversation in great contrast to the uncivilized
surroundings. But spirits high.

David Herbert's love for Morocco abounding. When I asked
what country he would like to inhabit if he could not remain
here, he gasped. He loves the Moors.

Arrival at Portuguese sixteenth- or seventeenth-century
Jewish town of Mogador. Pink and white castellated walls. The
Tosca-esque seventeenth-century ramparts with a twin-towered
archway and simple symmetrical ramps create shadows like
modern abstract paintings — the whole very much like de
Staël — in white, biscuit and browns. Town dotted with tall

ferns, growing like magnolia, and rows of argana, a sort of thin, monkey-puzzle tree.

Sudden great enthusiasm, beautiful old city with everything in harmony, even the modern, white buildings have the same feeling as the old. Lots of exciting pictures taken, and back to a pleasant, comfortable, modest hotel for lunch and siesta before further sightseeing. White-veiled women with black shuttered faces flee the evil eye of the camera but were so entranced listening to the theatre music coming from a *Les Forains* circus tent that they became oblivious of one. With great excitement, I clicked until dark.

Have been reading Volume II of Harold Nicolson's *Diaries* with as much pleasure as I read his first. I wonder why, in spite of being told again and again by his friends, James Pope-Hennessy and others, what a fine fellow he is, I've never liked the man.

Once more he shows himself to be an honest, good character, sensitive to others, candid about himself. He is never vulgar, and always has an eye for the comic. Often he is able in the written word to move me; in fact I finished this book in a blur of tears.

But when scrutinizing the photographs I again see that I am as put off by his physical appearance there, as I am in life. How unfair this is. But the Kewpie-doll mouth, the paradoxical moustache, the corpulence of hands and stomach all give me a *frisson* and there is no getting over the fact that I could never get to know him well enough to become a close friend. Sad, because he could have been a help and guide and an influence for the better.

Reddish: June 1967

Monday morning my breakfast is brought in — tea, charcoal biscuits, yogurt and the papers. I am looking out of the window at the green scene when I hear that war has started in the Middle East. Israel and Egypt are each saying the other was the first to be the aggressor.

The awful sinking dread surged through from the nape of the neck to the solar plexus. At once one thinks, not of the suffering, the pain, the killings in the far land, but selfishly of home and oneself. If the war spreads we are liable to become involved, even if only remotely, by, say, the rationing of fuel. It seems such a little time ago that we were doing all we could to scrounge an extra can of petrol. But the continual dread ... the encroaching anxiety.

Miraculously the Israelis have overthrown the Egyptians. Against all odds, with brilliant tactics and fierce fighting, they have brought about in three days a complete reversal of the Middle-East picture.

No one can be more delighted than our neighbour up the valley — Anthony Eden.

There was quite an extraordinary atmosphere of joy and celebration in the pretty Georgian house at Alvediston that Clarissa and Anthony have recently bought. Despite his plastic duct and continuous fever, Anthony had reached the age of seventy. It was his birthday and the events of the last week were a wonderful present. They have meant that, in principle, Anthony's much criticized policy on Suez, and his distrust of Nasser, were correct. Clarissa, generally so cold and reserved, admitted this evening that she was 'stewed'. She was enchanting in her gaiety and, in an aside of happiness, said: 'I never thought Anthony would live long enough to see himself proved right.'

Anthony, sunburnt and wearing a marrow-coloured velvet dinner-suit, seemed the picture of health and radiance. He was surrounded by his loyal *confrères*, and a few members of his family. Bobbity Salisbury made a speech that was eulogistic but neither embarrassing nor sentimental. Oliver Lyttleton, whose desire to amuse has increased with the years to the extent that he is a real bore, made one funny joke. The evening was a great success. A surprising group: the Lambtons motored from London; Lord Scarborough came from Yorkshire; Nicholas and other young Edens; Lord Brooke; Ronnie Tree; Anthony and Dot Head; and the Hoffs[7] (whom I brought).

Nicholas handed round tulip-shaped glasses of Elizabethan Kümmel! This was real dynamite! It tasted like aquavit, and took the breath away as it went down the throat. Bottles of champagne popped, and the gathering was very English, understated and poignant.

MY LAST ASCOT

Old age creeps upon me in many indefinable ways. In spite of exercises and massage from Charlotte Gaffran, and being stretched and manipulated by Svenson, my back aches and I am apt to walk upstairs more slowly. I realize I am not as young as I was. Fewer things seem to give me pleasure. Lately I have felt a restlessness that is most unwelcome. I have noticed on the faces of older people the terrible look of empty boredom. Is this coming my way? The only thing to dispel it is work and, thank heavens, I have my painting (and sometimes my writing) to keep the heavier hours at bay.

As a snobbish boy I was always disappointed when my mother's request for tickets to the Royal Enclosure at Ascot

---

[7] Raimund von Hofmannsthal and his wife (Lady) Elizabeth.

were turned down. But the slap in the face came back again and again from Lord Churchill on behalf of the King. However, nowadays anyone who can pay the few guineas necessary is welcomed, and with the opening of the flood-gates that allowed in Jack Hylton, Binkie Beaumont and any little starlet, I was given the OK. But it was too late. By the time I got there the grand ladies in their fantastic dresses and the exclusiveness had all gone.

The Ascot weeks that I spent, in the pleasant company of Mrs Nancy Lancaster, were really rather an effort. I know nothing whatever about racing, and I was soon bored and tired.

The rules have now changed. You need not buy a Royal Enclosure ticket for a whole week. So, for one day, I thought it might be fun. I went under the best auspices, with Jakie and Chiquita Astor, whom I love. He, as a member of the Jockey Club, can make things easy. We had a delightful lunch at their flat. The car journey was enjoyable until the queue started, half an hour away from the course. Then all sorts of forgotten snobberies rose to the surface; unimportant things assumed importance; our eventual arrival on the course was perfectly timed so that we saw the royal procession coming towards us. Some people with a banner were running in front of the oncoming horses. 'Stop the murder in Vietnam.' The police, like bioscope cops, were slow off the mark.

The colour of Royal Ascot has changed — Edwardian Ascot must have been entirely pastel coloured. But this was a transformation that I enjoyed. Everywhere there were large touches of brilliant magenta, orange and viridian. The Maharaja of Jaipur in a marvellous turban of ochre and scarlet. Yet the retina-irritant mutation of the plastic and the nylon looked crummy in the outdoors; the crocheted shift, the mini skirts and little-girl fashions were hardly right. But then I was not right.

Loelia Westminster gave me a look of surprise. 'What are *you* doing here?' She may well ask. I suddenly realized I wasn't enjoying myself and that I was only pretending. It was tedious to go into that Holy of Holies, the Jockey Club restaurant for a short drink of iced coffee and to hear Lady Sefton abuse her husband. The only diversion was losing each way on Mrs Englehard's horse. The sight of the French Ambassadress wearing an art nouveau picture-hat adorned with water lilies was the only fashion note that gave me a slight tremor.

But I was not diverted in any way and all I could think of was getting away and leaving before the last race in order to miss the worst of the traffic. My only crumb of pleasure was the company of my friends.

I returned home crushed with fatigue, and, worse, fear that my powers of appreciation of this form of entertainment had entirely gone. For me at my time of life to go off to such a function was perhaps asking for trouble. At sixty-three I must seek other excitements.

Corfu, on the Wrightsman yacht: July

The Greek royal family came on board for lunch. (Evelyn Waugh once wrote that the presence of royalty was like heavy thunder in the air.)

The King, very boyish, with puppy fat, came from Athens. He was grateful to be asked to take off his coat. His Queen, pretty complexioned, but as yet too young to show any character, was dressed in a most uneventful way. I have Queen Frederica on my left and her giggling daughter Sophie on my right. Sophie is easy to talk to, with bulging low cheeks, silken hair, drooping eyelids, button-mushroom nostrils, baby teeth, and pretty eyes. Her unmarried sister Irene is the more serious of the two and is a good pianist. Queen Frederica is deaf but I have her better ear. She talks of her vegetarianism. It started because she had seen so much suffering, and did not wish to inflict more on animals, fish, or anything that loved its mother. Much laughter. What about whitebait? She was surprised at our reaction, but has the sense to laugh at herself. 'I did not like my mother,' she added. She said that taking drugs was like having a glimpse of heaven, but paying with shoddy money. It should only be done in isolation. She said she had been called Fascist yet had worked on our side against the Germans during the war. The British papers had been monstrous, but she thought the people were sympathetic.

The Queen related being 'set upon' while walking with Princess Sophie outside Claridges and how shaken they had both been. As she walked on in a dignified way, her daughter had told her what was happening. 'Two are on the ground and now they are closing in on us.' They walked faster and only when in the mews at the back of the Italian Embassy did they run and ring a doorbell. This was how Marti Stevens, the actress whose doorbell it was, learned the story of the life of the Queen of Greece. The police and embassy attaches had eventually come to their rescue.

Then Queen Frederica heard the King talking about the revolution in Greece. He had been in his private cinema watching a Rock Hudson film. He had hated it so much that he decided to stay and see another film. By remaining so long he probably saved himself from being hijacked on the road to his country home. In the middle of the night his secretary telephoned to say there was a revolution. 'Who are they?' 'Don't know.' He telephoned to his mother and spoke in whispers. Guns put to his door. 'We are here to protect you.'

Army officers, some of whom he did not know, were the instigators.

Fortunately there was no bloodshed. Matters had been cleverly organized and soon the whole excitement had died down. Then they began to realize that changes had to be made; that the regime could have turned Communist and the whole family put behind the Iron Curtain.

SELF-ANALYSIS

I have not allowed my mind to be trained, or my interests to broaden. I am in many ways the same person I was forty years ago. But with a slowing down. I can't take in as much as I could. I learn nothing new. I get tired more easily, and bored. Even my ambitions are less than they were. I don't seem to have any plan to do anything that I have not tried before. If I survive, I may publish more diaries, but the fount of inspiration for an original book seems to have dried up, and the chances of writing for the theatre are becoming rarer. I may possibly do a bit more painting. However much I am interested in today's phenomenon there are positive signs that I have become part of an older generation with its tired attitude and approach.

I don't really feel that I am ever going to come into my own, to justify myself and my existence by some last great gesture. I am likewise certain that nothing I have done is likely to live long after me.

I have got to the point where I know I should relax, calm down, read more, and prepare for retirement. But I realize how little accustomed I am to living without surface excitements. The whole problem of the future is one of anxiety.

The other day when discussing with Eileen the problem of whether or not to spend £2,000 on an addition to the house in the country I said: 'I'd like to have the benefit of the change as soon as possible because God knows how many years I will be spared. Any minute I may get an unpleasant shock and a tax man come along.' Eileen said: 'You've probably got another twenty years.' How appalling! I don't necessarily want to take my own life, but I don't want to have to hang on patiently bearing the humiliations, the lonelinesses, the discomforts of decrepitude.

Yet perhaps this is not for one to decide. My father was sad, bored and alone in his late sixties, and my mother was brave about all the physical disabilities she had to put up with until she was nearly ninety. I am glad that, unlike poor Rex Whistler, I was allowed to survive the last war, but I don't really find myself enjoying life today as much as I did before.

Randolph Churchill, looking old and grey, like a haggard hawk, has been on the brink of death for three years. The other night he told me that he was now happier than he had ever been. He was at last doing something that justified his life — his book on his father, the best thing he had ever done, his contribution to the world; the fact that he was no longer restless was balm to him. I am sure he was being sincere, but it is hard to believe. His eyes look so abysmally sad.

THE THEATRE

The theatre is another form of enforced entertainment that I am finding hard to enjoy. Early on in life it was enough for me just to watch the curtain rise on an illuminated set, and to peer at the make-up on the performers' faces. Now this is not so. The well-known situations, the clichés, and the presentation of such conventionality in the usual commercial play does not give me anything but excruciating uneasiness.

I have become expert at quitting the theatre at the first interval. But after the trouble, time and expense of getting there by 'curtain-up', this is not a satisfactory way of spending the evening.

On one occasion, however, I was utterly contented. This was at Hampstead when Roy Dotrice gave an extraordinary portrayal of old age in a one-part play about John Aubrey of Broadchalke. This piece, derived from Aubrey's diaries, showed the old professor working, going through domestic chores and thinking aloud about life on the last day of his life. Dotrice's understanding, his love and sympathy for old age, was one of the best pieces of histrionic art I have ever seen. It was an exquisite pleasure.

The strange play *Rosencrantz and Guildenstern are Dead* also gave me a lift. It embodied in a different, oblique way, the essence of the theatre. The romanticism, even the mysticism, of the players and the innate poetry made it a rare experience.

CHRISSIE GIBBS

September 1967

Chrissie Gibbs is a delightful, intelligent and extremely well-informed young man.

When he asked me to have dinner I thought it would be a quiet one with him. I returned to Pelham extremely late, in a state of near collapse, having been out all day. I rang to ask if it would matter my being a little late. 'Not at all — take it easy.'

On arrival I found Jane Ormsby Gore, with her baby, Saffron, lying in a shopping basket. She was calm and sad about the tragic accident that had killed her mother four days before. She spoke sympathetically about the misery that her father must face each time some new aspect of his loss occurs. The snapshots that he took on that last Sunday's tea-party, at which I was a guest, will one day be returned from the printers. Chrissie hustled about his dark panelled rooms doing nothing in particular and certainly never settling down to talk. Half an hour later Michael Wishart, freshly out of a nursing-home, came to call for Jane. She snatched up the basket and they disappeared. 'Mick's coming to dinner,' said Chrissie, 'bringing Marianne Faithfull, but I can't think where they are.' At 10.15 they appeared. Mick was in a gold brocade coat with tight, coffee-coloured trousers. He shrugged a bit, made no pretence of manners, and settled down to look at a picture book. Marianne, with white suety face, the usual drowned-blonde hair and smudged eyes, her dress torn under the arm, fluttered, and made 'groovy' conversation. Also present, by now, was Prince Stanislas, or some such name. I remembered seeing him two years ago at a freak Dufferin party as a huge white and black Hamlet, wearing, in spite of the heat, a heavy, black cape. He looked extremely self-conscious and po-faced. Tonight he was still dressed as Hamlet, with strips of sequins on his blouse and his sleeves painted psychedelically in silver, magenta and gold. He showed a large, white décolletage, a vast Adam's apple, huge white hands covered with rings, Byzantine-black page-boy hair, white face and potato nose. Throughout the long evening he spoke not at all.

In spite of the impediment in his speech, the most articulate person there was Robert Fraser. He has the usual pallor, the five-o'clock shadow, the tie badly in need of a pull up, and hair.

At 11.30 pm we went off in taxis to the Bagdad House restaurant in Fulham Road. Here, in the club-like atmosphere of the basement, we found others of the gang. Mark Parker, more rodentlike than ever with his greasy blond hair over his nose; Michael Wishart, looking as if he needed to go back to the nursing-home; the youngest Tennant girl dressed like an aged 1920s figure with dark glasses, frizzed hair, a mini skirt over thick, purple, woollen stockings and rows of clairvoyant's beads. Also now present were Jane Ormsby Gore with her husband, Michael Rainey. He was asleep, 'out', with his head on a shoulder; nearby, oblivious of the flashing lights and roar of a juke box, was the baby, Saffron, in the shopping basket.

I tried to talk to Mick. He shrugged, twitched his eyes, contorted his mouth and screwed up his face. He was hungry. He wanted 'fewd'. Little plates of mush were brought. He put a cake of pap into his huge mouth. I was, by now, in a trance of fatigue. Robert Fraser extolled the virtues of Andy Warhol's *Chelsea Girls* film. Wouldn't I like to come and see it? He had it at home. It runs for four hours. I wondered if I should be a devil and make a night of it. But no, I hadn't the strength. I said: 'If you'll excuse me.' It was one o'clock when I left to walk home up the deserted Fulham Road, leaving the night to the rest of them to turn into something or nothing.

I'd never met Princess Alice, Countess of Athlone before, but lately, going through early bound magazines, I had seen pictures of her at her wedding. I was struck by the tininess of her waist and the *potelé* little bosom and rounded hips that were pushed out from the corset. Now today the Princess, playing croquet under the cedars of Lebanon at Wilton, was disguised as an eighty-year-old lady.

The remains of beauty are still there, thought the waist has gone; together with her porcelain complexion.

But unlike most royalty, and perhaps she has the advantage of being very 'minor', she has a directness that is healthy, and her shyness is well under control.

The Pembrokes keep up the tradition of the Edwardian house-party and had assembled twelve for this weekend, which was now, on Sunday evening, at a low ebb, half of the guests having departed. The croquet over, we were relaxing in the library having a drink before changing. Princess Alice talked on her 'Topic A' which was Queen Victoria.

The following points interested me. The Queen's children were all very much in awe of this fearsome little figure. Since it was always being drummed into them that they must behave well in front of her, when she appeared they quaked. But she was easy and good-humoured, laughed a lot and had two long, birdlike teeth in front that appeared whenever she was amused. Princess Victoria, known as 'The Snipe', inherited them.

The Queen was very clean and always smelt refreshingly of rosewater. She was often making a hat, platting straw together, and the Princess Alice was furious at having to wear this hat which she considered hideous.

The Queen had no figure, just an avalanche of basalt black with little, white lawn collar and cuffs that were immaculate. I think the word for the neckpiece was 'tucker'. She did not wear it high round the neck in the fashion of the time, but was quite *décolleté*, and therefore dowdy.

At Windsor, Balmoral and Osborne there was always too much food. The sideboards were heavy with cold and hot meats, fowls and capons. There were always two soups, clear and thick; fish and eggs, and so much for the servants to take away. Such a waste!

Part IV: Behind the Iron Curtain, 1967

WARSAW

September 1967

First visit to the large, sprawling, creamish-coloured Wilanow Palace. Originally built for Jan Sobieski in the seventeenth century, it was rehashed in the 1840s for the Potockis with Victorian chutney-coloured doors, poor frescoes and indiscriminate decoration, stucco, statues, and busts. Some of the tall-ceilinged rooms were impressively hung with Genoese velvet. There were galleries of archaic family portraits of a certain individual Polish charm, the women with long, pointed faces like Dolly Radziwill, and pretty costume nonsenses of sun bonnets, scarlet or black bows, and odd uses of brocade. The use of candles in sconces at intervals on bookcases is an idea I'd like to copy. A fearsome bathroom decorated with cheap silk in bosses and peacock's feathers. Some good French furniture, boulle, lacquer. The rooms were all carefully redecorated with great taste and bravery. Although the exterior was rather sad, and the gardens badly planted with salvias and other Victoriana, it was pleasant to walk on the terraces and in the water gardens.

We saw the amazingly reconstructed old city, medieval Rynek, copied faithfully from documents of Belotto, so that it is now just as it used to be before.

We did not realize what terrible damage the bombing had done, or maybe we had just forgotten the horror, until we were shown by the National Museum people a film of just how determined the Germans were that the city of Warsaw should be completely wiped out. The devastation of the raids was later followed by the German soldiers setting fire with flame-throwers to any building that remained standing; ninety-nine per cent of the city was destroyed. The film was so impressive, so nightmarish, that it has made all the difference to one's point of view about the things one sees today. That the Poles should immediately start rebuilding the city as it once was, was an act of faith that is quite unbelievable. At the moment there is still little enough to make life seem easy, but their faith in the future guided them through a terror and misery that few other countries have ever endured.

Then to Lazienki Palace, in a park facing a lake, a fairy-tale palace with colonnaded wings, and two gilded balconies. The Germans had done their best to dynamite everything that could be valuable, the ceilings, frescoes, statuary, but the reconstruction has been a miracle, not only of dedication and love but of taste. A small, intimate hall, white and grey marble with heavy stucco ceiling, leads to a small, all-Delft room and a small green silk room with family portraits; garlands of wild flowers decorate the frames of engravings; then a yellow velvet room; and a ballroom of sunlit whiteness.

Tuesday, September 5th

8.30 am bus start. I could not read and after two hours the motion of the bus made me feel ill. The towns had displayed their bombed desolation. The scenery through which we passed was deeply depressing. The countryside showed that the Poles have never progressed in the tilling of their land since the Middle Ages, and that modern machines are not welcomed even if they could be paid for. Horses draw the carts which, as a concession to modernization, have Michelin tyres on their wheels. Thatched *chatas* falling down; weeds everywhere; poor soil.

We followed the Vistula for miles of flat decay. Even the cemeteries are untended. Few pets, one or two dogs, not a cat in sight. Such an extra expense is discouraged.

The day was pastel-coloured and hazy with filtered sun. Our first stop was a large house at Pulawy: gothicized inside with iron staircases and tall windows; outside a battlement. A walk through the park was made charming by hundreds of young school-children, all looking the same. They were blond with blunt features, clean, well shod, well dressed and well mannered, being tended by kind women who appeared to have been gathering mushrooms. But the general poverty is disturbing.

Lunch at Renaissance Square in Kazimierz/Dolny, where there is a façade elaborately sculpted with animals and people reminiscent of Hardwick. Then an appallingly long drive to Lancut. The scenery more congenial. The landscape less flat, richer, greener and better tended. Daylight fading upon pretty scenes of haymaking, and strong aromas.

Disappointing to find Lancut was not in its own park, but right in a town. There was a hideous garden, and, to match, a hideous façade. The castle covered with tin advertisement signs.

Count and Countess Roman Potocki came down to greet us; the squire with hat and stick, she in false pearls with a shopping bag and a twitch. The hall was unbelievably ugly; the reception rooms and the corridors were beyond belief a disappointment. Admittedly all the good furniture had been removed and taken away in nine train-loads during the war, but even so what was left was vulgar and coarse.

It was sad to see the place in the care of a museum custodian and his staff. Many housemaids now sweep and dust for the State. They have no resentment of the former owners; in fact, the family photographs are exhibited proudly and so great the interest that in a country where there are few cars as many as 5,000 visitors come on a Sunday.

I could not help thinking that the reputation that had gone before was grossly exaggerated. The grandeur only asserted itself as one saw the first-floor rooms: the bedroom-boudoir of the Countess Betka Potocka, the ballroom like a stage set, the library, the billiard room; and, above all, the 1914 theatre. This was built by a Viennese architect; there were garlands of double rows of illuminated chandelier drops hanging from the ceiling; and on stage a ravishing set of painted roses for a musical comedy.

The visit to the coachhouses was really exciting; beautiful carriages of every sort, each with its own personality, black and brown veneers, black leather, shining harnesses; and sledges; all smelling of horse.

In strange contrast our rooms in the so-called 'Palace' Hotel were primitive. No room had its own bath or lavatory, and tonight no room had any running water. How to wash one's teeth? How to go to the loo? The twenty of us all took the crisis extremely well. When one thinks of how Madame Patino Ortiz would not dream of going without even a bottle of mineral water, one has to laugh.

Wednesday, September 6th

The journey to Cracow was exceedingly long and tedious. The countryside (with the Vistula popping up — very flat — every now and again) was not particularly pleasing although happily the earth seemed richer, the badly tended crops healthier, and the effect greener.

On the streets the people looked much less miserable than in Russia, but the suffering is excruciating. Before dinner we went to have a drink with the Roman Potockis, who would have been heirs to Lancut but for the Russians. The staircase leading to their room was of a squalor unimaginable, permeated with the smells of a restaurant on the ground floor and the nearby refuse bins. The room that he shares with his wife and children is only theirs in the afternoon. In it there is the lavabo, and the kitchen sink and stove; the bed of madame is pushed behind a screen and monsieur's bed becomes a sofa during the day. The room contains many mementoes. Some beautiful furniture, a few good paintings, and photograph albums to remind them of former glory.

However, pity must not be felt. They could live elsewhere if they wished. But they find Paris life insupportable. Here at least they are cheerful.

Friday, September 8th

Today was a comparative treat, for we started our sightseeing at the reasonable hour of 9.30. Just to say that we went to a college, an art museum, the souks, the large 'Place', the Wawel, and five churches does not give any idea of the physical effort needed to carry out this venture. The bus could not be found, a guest could not be found. We walked and walked, and did our best to behave well; only the art-guide lost his temper.

To see Wawel Castle and Wawel Cathedral was rewarding. The castle with its sixteenth-century colonnaded courtyard is the former seat of the kings of Poland, and contains among its treasures the famous collection of Flemish tapestries woven in Brussels in the sixteenth century and displayed here with impeccable care and taste. Inside there are marble-floored rooms, leather walls, heavy gilt and painted ceilings, huge bronze chandeliers, dark Renaissance tables, throne chairs and, above all, the tapestries — hundreds of them in dozens of rooms. I, no connoisseur, was impressed by the colours still being so fresh, by the bird's-egg blue among the silver and rose threads, the biblical figures over life-size, and the scenes of animal jungle life in a fantasized Africa.

Tents captured from the Turks at the Battle of Vienna in 1683 were part of a permanent exhibition of Oriental art. They were embroidered, appliqued with an extraordinary variety of designs on the same theme, rose colours predominating; stylized flowers with black-dotted centres. Altogether they created a magic that is beyond description; revelation was enough.

In the museum in the vaults of the castle there was much to see: armour, Meissen, Chinese and Japanese porcelain, swords of unparalleled magnificence, all beautifully shown.

Wawel Cathedral houses bright shining marble tombs of the kings of Poland from the earliest times with their individuality intact. One fifteenth-century king, having the nose of my mother's family, prompted a closer look.

The visit to the Collegium Maius was of special interest. It was thrilling to see so many beautifully decorated medieval rooms overlooking a large, dun-coloured opera set of a court. They were wonderful and smelt of wax. A smaller room, M. Lerone's study, contained odd mathematical and scientific instruments, and a wooden statue of King Casimir, the founder of the college, who was considered to be one of the best mathematicians and physicists of his day in the world. The former college now houses the University Museum and has a remarkable collection of astrolabes and globes, and shown to their greatest advantage on a marvellous staircase are beautiful petit-point tapestries. Many of the exhibits are connected with the scientific research carried out by Copernicus.

As we stepped outside we were almost drenched by the water jets which were cleaning the building in De Gaulle's honour. The General was to make a speech in the glorious lecture hall.

Then to the square, vaster than any in Europe; flower markets; Victorian souks in which, sadly, one had no desire to buy a thing.

The Eglise Notre Dame is as grand as any cathedral. We heard the trumpeter in the tower sound the midday notes; inside there were many peasants with handkerchiefs on their heads and nuns wearing fantastic coifs. They contributed to the splendour of this tall, forest-like building with green fourteenth-century windows, blue vaulted ceiling, huge altar piece, and wonderful carving.

The afternoon took us to the enormous eighteenth-century collection made and given to the country by the Czartoryski family — who at one time had everything and now nothing. The pearl of the collection was the painting by Leonardo of the woman holding an ermine, a beautiful young mistress of one of the Sforzas.

But how much sightseeing can one take in? What about the five churches to see? One had a pulpit like a golden ball with cherubs peeping out from a silver sheet, another was a huge, gloomy, grey church, and then there was an art nouveau one with lilies and nasturtiums in the stained glass and on the child's-illustration-like walls.

The huge Gustave Doré edifice of the castle of Pieskowa Skala, twenty-five miles outside Cracow on a high mountain crag in a most beautiful valley, raised our spirits at the end of an exhausting day.

I feel there is no hope for the Poles. They are sandwiched between Russia and Germany, a helpless situation. They are sentimental about the past but cannot create a style which is new and modern.

I asked one of the most mouse-like of my fellow travellers what had most impressed her on the trip, and she answered, without hesitation, the 'hauteur' of the Poles. It is extraordinary that, in the face of the most appalling anxiety, disaster, and poverty, they continue to have courage and hope.

There was little time for sleep before a 6.45 am call, and the start of a long day in the motor, three hundred and more kilometres to Brno in Czechoslovakia, where we were to spend several days.

I had decided after this to cut short my trip and escape the week in Germany. It was a pity to miss the unique opportunity of seeing the state of that unhappy land, but I could not take in all those palaces en route — saturation point had been reached.

CZECHOSLOVAKIA

September 9th

The sun has gone; a wet day. The troupe all appear in tweed, some with shooting hats. We drive in the bus for one hour in mist. Terribly ugly suburbs of Brno. Then into a countryside which at least looks prosperous in comparison to Poland.

First stop the eighteenth-century castle of Milotice, which once belonged to the Serenyi family. Approached over a bridge carrying huge stone sphinxes and urns. Inside the atmosphere was one of a large country house full of sporting charm, stuffed birds, deer and antelope; a good simple staircase, Biedemeier furniture; one room decorated entirely like a scrapbook, very pretty in its yellow-green varnish. All that was missing was the family, who are now probably living in a garret.

Next stop Buchlovice, until 1939 belonging to the Berchtold family. This is a triumph of ground planning, with crescents complementing crescents, ingenious vistas of steps and statue-decorated balustrades; and delightful wrought-iron work; every sort of tree flourished in the garden and park, and peacocks strutted round the ornamental pond. The whole effect was like a Bakst creation for a ballet of *The Sleeping Beauty*.

Prague

We visited the Jewish quarter and went into two synagogues; one was an early one, the other in memory of the Jews massacred in Czechoslovakia. At first I thought the walls were made of neatly textured stone, but on closer inspection I saw the names of the thousands and thousands who were exterminated. Nearby the Jewish cemetery remains intact, a wholesale mess of broken stones left by the Germans as a relic of an extinct race. It seems that the Germans never mention this; not even the children. 'Be a sport. Come, forget it,' is their attitude.

I felt sorry for the group as the rain-drenched bus, steam clouding its windows, turned the corner and was out of sight on its way to East Germany. I was not ashamed of having chickened out. In fact Liliane de Rothschild admitted I was intelligent. I smiled and waved with genuine gaiety.

But left alone I didn't feel completely at ease; so many unexpected things can happen in this strange, mysterious town.

However, things did not turn out badly. I kept my appointment with Mr Liehm who was going to show me previews of two 'important' new Czech films. The first was about the beastliness of four school-children to another of their class, the message being don't turn the other cheek, meet bad with worse. It was a cruel picture, beautifully produced in every way, an honest piece of art. The second, by Forman, was brilliantly funny, cruel and tragic, a satire on the government, who were seen as a bunch of bungling, incompetent, dishonest firemen. The Firemen's League were to give a goodbye present to their former director, an eighty-three-year-old peasant dying of cancer. They organized a ball with tombola and beauty contest. The rustic ruggedness of the ball was hilariously shown, the beauties appalling and the tombola prizes ghastly. Suddenly the old man's house catches fire and is destroyed. He is brought to the ball in his pyjamas. He shall be given all the tombola tickets, but who had taken the bottle of brandy? Who took that hunk of meat? Who took that box of chocolates? The entire tombola had been stolen. What can we say to the people? They will accuse us. This will ruin our reputation and reputation is more important than honesty. When the prize is presented to the aged director he opens his leather and velvet case — this prize too had been stolen.

Liehm considers Prague today one of the most progressive capitals in the world. Nobody has any belief in the government. In 1945 they put up a poor resistance to Russia compared with Poland.

Everybody defies the bumbling gangsters. Nobody obeys the rules, not even the police; but matters have reached a pitch where the future might be dangerous and a return to Stalinist censorship, prisons, and worse precipitated. The younger generation have no fear; they have zest and vitality, but their audacity might have to be curbed in case they go too far.

Liehm is a firebrand. A critic and a writer, he runs an uncensored weekly magazine. He took me around the Kafka sights.

One has only to be a few days in Prague before fully realizing the genius of Kafka. The air is impregnated with his spirit. Thirty years ago he wrote of everything that has happened here and is happening today. It is a town that is locked and has only the wrong keys, the keys that won't fit the locks; things are not ruined and spoiled so much as baulked.

New York: November 18th

Noted the air so clear and bright. The sunset gaudy red. The illuminations well-polished diamonds. Everything has tremendous sharpness, a sequin glitter. Grand Central Station is the pinnacle ending Park Avenue's long, light-spattered stretch. In only a year many new, even more modern, apartments appear in a city that looks cleaner than it is.

The younger generation think differently from their parents; the hippie mentality is here, even among those that are not actually hippies. Young American men have long hair. Girls go out with negroes; negroes go everywhere. The dances are absolute jungle rites; the dancers pay little attention to one another except perhaps to embrace when the ritual is over. Any sort of clothing goes.

'The Electric Circus' a psychedelic playground with Gustave Doré flashing, changing colours, moving pictures, amplified sound in a grotto: totally experimental and unconventional; makes one feel old and square, and a sightseer of a different century.

A nice compliment from Marianne Moore, who said to me: 'You're a great example to us all. You're so modest. You exact the most of yourself.'

Since her 'inconvenient' birthday (she was recently eighty) she has had a kaleidoscope of a life. After a while she says she hopes to be 'thinned out'.

NEW YORK: MARGOT FONTEYN

November 1967

Eileen has a great deal more patience than I have. She has many uses for it, being victim, on the telephone, of the vagaries of the rich and spoilt people who speak more bluntly to her than to me. But even Eileen got exasperated with Margot Fonteyn.

Months ago Diana Vreeland, editor-in-chief of *Vogue* magazine, said she wanted a pictorial feature showing the greatness of the dancer 'as a woman'. The article to accompany the pictures was to be written by Marguerite Duras. But Margot kept postponing the engagement with me. She is, admittedly, tremendously busy. She knows her days of retirement are not far off, and she is making as many appearances as she can possibly fit in in all parts of the world.

It is a bore to be photographed. But the prevarications were endless. Margot would be in Paris between the 3rd and the 19th, if I'd come over, but she couldn't pose on the 4th, 5th, 6th, 7th, 8th, 11th, etc., etc. Then she was going to Sweden, then Texas, but she didn't know when that would be.

Suddenly she was completely out of touch. Eventually we tried to reach her through her mother and through her chauffeur. I then sent a frenzied telegram to Diana in New York.

Vogue paid the fare for Margot to come from Dallas and sent a car to the airport to meet her, by which time I was in New

York too. She rang to know if she could be photographed in the home of Trumble Barton where she was staying, but this was not allowed.

Margot arrived at my hotel quite punctually, very staccato and jolly. She said she was sorry I'd got the impression she didn't particularly want to be photographed by me; more than anyone else she wanted me.

Margot, at over fifty, still possesses the line and movement of youth. Her legs are long and straight, and go into ballet positions which look odd when she wears a very 'way out' St Laurent evening dress. Her spirit shines through like a blade of young grass.

She is totally an artist. To those who have known her well all through the early stages, and have influenced her in one way or another, her blossoming into the ballerina assoluta and becoming a legend must be very gratifying.

Part V: Hither and Thither, 1968-70

January 5th, 1968

The building alterations at Reddish were considered to be of a minor character until the men started to hack down an inside wall. Then one thing led to another. It seems that if the alterations had not been done, i.e. the creation of a 'landing' library, and the addition of guest bathrooms, the landing floor would sooner or later have caved in anyway; the boards had become rotten and were resting on the water pipes. The cisterns in the attic were about to burst and had to be replaced. When the faulty ones were brought down they were found to be filled with the bones of rats, birds, cats, and other animals, and with horror we realized that for years we had been drinking the water in which these bodies had been decomposing.

Now, when the main work is nearing its end, we are told that the roof above the garage may fall in any day, that certain walls are being pushed out too far, and that a perilously leaning chimney-stack must be dismantled, brick by brick and put back again.

All of this is a very boring way of spending a lot of money at a time when the country has been brought to economic chaos, and we are all fearful of what the new Labour Chancellor may introduce in the way of taxes, squeezes and restrictions.

I am advised about my finances by an old man who must surely be left over from the time of Dickens. He does not seem to me to have the sort of fighting qualities which I would have thought necessary in such a difficult taxation time. I am in the hopeless condition of knowing nothing about my own money affairs.

I rely upon Eileen to be level-headed enough to say when I am in a really serious jam. As it is, it is a battle to make money enough to pay the income tax. This year has been a poor one financially. The result is that I now feel extremely wary of spending even the ordinary cash for everyday expenses. In comparison to some, I suppose I am well off. But by the standards of most solvent people, my existence is pretty precarious. With God on my side, I may continue to make enough to keep going to the end. But it takes a jolt like a transatlantic journey to make one realize that one can lose sense of everything except one's immediate surroundings. Other people's currency seems remote, and values are merely relative to one's immediate needs. Thus a peseta is a windfall to a starving Spaniard, while a hundred thousand bucks is chicken feed to a Hollywood agent.

A few hours after my arrival in New York I was in the middle of the sort of activity that doesn't come my way at home: a decorator needs materials; a man wants designs for carpets; someone is interested in the idea of my doing a club restaurant. Here, suddenly, I'm in touch with business. In London I'm guarded against the outside world, but here I realize I must step out of my little orbit and see what is happening.

An evening with David Bailey was a revelation. At thirty he has made a fortune as a photographer and owns eight different companies in Switzerland and Lichtenstein. He is on the ball in a way that it is intelligent for an artist to be, and, of course, he has a very good accountant. I would like to be able to learn a few of his tricks. It would not mean that I become less of an artist, but more sensible about important practical matters and less worried when Mr Blick, the builder, says that it will cost £250 to renovate the garage roof.

If I stay long in New York, the activities gang up on me with such speed that I forget the importance of taking time off to attend to the understanding of my money. As soon as I sense I am in a rut, either of illness, stagnation, or overwork, it is good for me to pull stumps and move on to get a different perspective.

Bora-Bora, Pacific Ocean: January, 1968

When I saw the Tahitian bungalow of bamboo and palm fronds in which I was to stay alone for three or four days, I felt utterly lost. Why had I come all this way to be trapped? Like many people I have a certain fear of being alone, although sometimes I like time off from people in my own house. However, the time passed quickly and agreeably, thanks partly to the calming atmosphere of this tiny, humid, tropical island in the middle of the Pacific, but mainly thanks to Jane Austen. Each time I returned from an expedition in or on the translucent sea, or returned from a meal of fruit, I became absorbed in the Bennett family. Their problems and their characteristics are so real that I am amused and fascinated, and not a little moved from time to time.

The villages are the same as those in almost every tropical part of the world, and the hotel is planned like others, large dining-room and office and thirty-three bungalows dotted among the coconut palms. All the lush, plummy vegetation makes the island look exactly like the eighteenth-century engravings done at the time of Captain Cook's voyages. The mountains are of basalt and have now acquired, after millions of years, very peculiar sawn-off, rather hideous, shapes. The grey summits may be in cloud, but the mountain-sides are sunny velvety green, covered with flowering trees, palms, bananas and mangoes, and bushy with coffee and vanilla.

The white coral reef seems miles away; inside the lagoon the waters are quite still and one can see the wonderful rainbow colours of the forests of coral and seaweed below.

My first morning glimpse was of an idyllic shore with white sands, a tangerine, lilac and rose sea, the blue sky filled with circling, shrieking, white birds — the terns, so named by Cook's botanist, Sir Joseph Banks. The water was almost rippleless, in fact it engulfed one like a caress. I ventured on a plastic floating mattress with a peephole to the deep through which I watched white and yellow fish darting in and out of the coral. By snorkelling extraordinary magical mysteries below the surface were revealed to me. The coral forests were of every variety of tree, some like firs, some windswept conifers, others yellow spiked, some dappled with purple, some like nuggets of gold. The pale grey and blue were like white icicles. At one's approach a complete cloud of brilliant blue fish with black spotted backs panicked and hurried for safety. A whole family of small white fish hovered near the white sandbed. A long, red-snouted fish looked as if he was out for trouble, and all the other fish rushed out of his way to take cover in a cranny or hole. Like every animal and insect, the lizards, birds and sea flies keep up a life-long battle for self-preservation.

AUSTRALIA

Sydney: January 1968

'Mr Beaton? Will you come this way please?' Embarrassing to be picked out for such unexpected and sudden attention, particularly as I was only on holiday; but I loved it! 'This way.' From the back of the economy class I was whisked through to an army of white-shirted, black-trousered customs officers. A Group Captain sent by Lord Casey to meet me. 'The Queen's photographer's luggage.'

I got into the waiting Rolls; conversation with an apple-cheeked ADC with a strong accent.

Pretty ironwork balconies on ramshackle early houses. The bridge, the new Opera House, boats bobbing up and down at the water's edge, the white, low-lying Admiralty House.

Another ADC at attention and there to greet me, the Caseys;[8] all the old English pomp — bow, bow, exchange of politeness, smiles, jokes, the grandchildren. A Monet scene through the windows; bright, ugly flowers, boats, modern skyscrapers forming a backcloth: an English countryhouse atmosphere.

The life at Admiralty House is so formal, so comfortable and conventional that one cannot break through to today. Competent secretaries enquire what help they can offer. They mean to carry through and they do. We meet punctually at mealtimes, ADCS prompt us, tell us where to sit: 'Your back will not be facing the window.' We make spasmodic conversation but it is never consecutive and often interrupted. No subject is therefore fully discussed. This makes for great frustration.

Having slept for ten hours at night I am asked: 'Would you care to rest this afternoon?' No, a plot has been brewing among the newly arrived guests. We would like to venture forth on our own to see the city, the suburbs, even go to a bathing beach. A limousine is ordered; a secretary directs the chauffeur, fills us in with information. This is the Library, the Wall Street area, King's Cross, the Soho part. This is the Chelsea or British part of the town, Kensington.

---

[8] Lord and Lady Casey.

It is impossible to get to grips with reality. The town is there in its physical sense but it seems there is no life. It is Australia Day, holiday weekend, and everyone has gone away. Hard to tell what sort of people live in the little houses, the new villas, the apartment houses, or the sleazy hotels; every part is abandoned as if there were a plague. It is only when we get to Bondi Beach that the real life is amusing to watch: so much activity; surfing, aquatic competitions of all kinds, life-savers rushing out to sea to protect people from currents, sharks and being battered on the rocks. Every colour of costume; a 'pop-art' kaleidoscope of young people, quite good-looking in an anonymous way, but no beauties, as you would see in Italy; everyone well disposed to each other; surprisingly, a lot of negroes and Chinese.

The limousine continues its tour. This is the Golf Club stretching for miles. Here the Park with the crowds listening to the soap-box preachers. We get down and mingle and listen, but time is short.

Over there is the Zoo; the new circular skyscraper; there the boats for the regatta, the tankers, the boat that brought soldiers back from Vietnam. We are due back to meet the grandchildren at five o'clock.

Later we got another car to take us to a park where koalas, wombats, and kangaroos are in a more or less natural setting. After twenty miles of suburbs, a side road brought us to mountainous, heavily wooded 'bush'. The animals were a bit squalid without sunlight. The glimpse was the nearest we have yet come to seeing something typically Australian.

The Art Gallery of New South Wales was very impressive and a selection of Chinese sculpture beautifully shown; women polo-riders and dancing girls, and a whole row of female musicians, now more beautiful than they must have been in their original crude colouring. Time has taken all but the most delicate traces of shrimp or lobster and fawn from the surface of these pale grey and pearly clays. There were good examples of the work of many modern painters. Most interesting, too, were the paintings by native aborigines.

At the back of this museum we saw the van which for four months will travel throughout Australia showing the people in many villages and outbacks their first original paintings. It was one of the signs of the determination of these people to make Australia into a great country of the future.

The Sydney Opera House makes all other opera houses look like coffers or kiosks, situated on this commanding promontory, dominating the city.

Canberra

The journey here to the seat of government was a revelation; no worry about whether we would miss the aeroplane, or be detained at customs: no lining up and waiting. The entire staff moves with Their Excellencies; some, including the chef, going on in advance.

The journey, over red, dusty, tufted earth and desert, takes only forty minutes. On arrival at Government House we go through the lodge and along an avenue of marvellously smelling pine trees. His Excellency is immediately at his desk. The guests investigate the low, rambling country house. It is all very comfortable and totally protected from the harshness of the world outside.

The heatwave continues. It is like a pall over the country. Today the temperature rose to 107 degrees. After a luncheon party for some visiting judges (luckily cold food), it was arranged that we should go and see an estancia — a sheep station.

Accompanied by the Comptroller, Colonel Rodriguez, we went off, over dirt-track roads, in the old-fashioned Rolls. Hermetically sealed inside, we were air-conditioned though the dust came through and up our noses. The poor chauffeur in heavy uniform was almost passing out. The countryside through which we drove was like Palestine; the eucalyptus in the distance looking like olive trees; rolling blue mountains and dun-coloured hills. The sheep looked pretty miserable in the drought. It was a surprise to find the person in charge of the station was a woman.

In the heatwave we went out to the various sheds. This is where the men are doing repair work to the cars. This is where the sheep are sheared, 200 a day, or, if they are very big ones, only 100. The place stank. But the stink and the heat here was as nothing compared with the next visit, a shed on which the sun poured, and which was filled with the pelts of sheep that had recently died in the drought and heat. The hot, rancid, pepper smell was too much to endure for long but the lady in charge was oblivious to heat and smell and continued to natter in her baby voice: 'I love it so much here that I never want to leave.'

One realized how at the mercy of the elements a great proportion of the earth's inhabitants are. If no rain comes then there is a general exodus; all the herds are driven away towards water. Sometimes the drought is so appalling that hundreds of thousands of animals die of heat and starvation.

Then the dryness is such that bush fires start. A woman in hospital, burnt beyond recognition, said, before she died, how grateful she was that all five of her children had survived. One woman, surrounded by fire, jumped into a water tank for safety but was boiled alive. The Australians do not seem to feel that their lot is a particularly hard one. They are not sorry for themselves.

It was a relief to come back to the luxuries of Government House.

Reddish

The news of Mrs Rhoda Templemore-Richardson's pathetic demise came the same morning that Timothy, the cat, fell into a tub of paraffin and weedkiller. His subsequent sufferings were dreadful to behold, with a raw backside and legs robbed of fur. But now, a week later, he seems to be recovering, thanks to the skill of a kind vet and the ministrations of the Smallpeices.[9] The cat, apart from the pain and stink, was intensely humiliated by his condition and his sorry appearance.

Mrs Templemore-Richardson was denied a quiet end to her life. She slaved so hard to look after her drunkard husband that she died suddenly of heart failure. She was a key figure in the village, a tragic woman whose love and public-spiritedness were a substitute for a happy private life.

Mrs Templemore-Richardson, a hoarder, left a houseful of hideous junk and old magazines; under her bed a trunk that had not been unpacked since she returned from Australia ten years ago.

Dr Burroughes, her closest friend and neighbour, informed us that she denied herself so much that she spent practically nothing on heat and food and had two hot baths a day to keep warm. Paradoxically she spent liberally on clothes and her house was filled with ensembles and hats by the hundreds which she never wore. Meanwhile, the husband is in hospital complaining that he is not given his two bottles of whisky a day.

---

[9] My gardeners, Mr and Mrs Smallpeice.

I found the Rhoda Templemore-Richardson's story, that of a too-good woman, very disturbing. If she had not taken her husband back after eighteen years, she might have had a much healthier and happier closing to her days. It seems saintliness doesn't pay off in this life.

THE QUEEN MOTHER TO LUNCH

Pelham Place: April 1968

Last time I was honoured in this way, Edith Sitwell was the *pièce de résistance*. Truman Capote had arrived an hour early and together with Eileen we had watched from a top window as a huge ambulance drove up to the house, and a pair of stalwart men moved to bring the poet out into the daylight. A pair of very long medieval shoes appeared, then a muffled figure and finally a huge, golden melon of a hat. Edith was wheeled into place and given two strong martinis. This time the mood struck me as much calmer.

The other guests arrived: Roy Strong in a psychedelic tie; Kirsty Hesketh, hatless and dressed by Courrèges like a child's idea of a primrose; Leo d'Erlanger, mundane in a black coat and wearing a hat which he subsequently forgot; Jakie Astor; Irene Worth, just right in non-colours; and Diana Cooper, casual, as beautiful as ever, with her habitual basket occupied by Doggie, the chihuahua.

The Queen Mother's huge limousine arrived and out stepped the smiling, delightful, familiar figure. She was dressed in brilliant puce and magenta. 'The last time ... poor Edith,' the delightful hesitancy, wistful eyes. 'How nice and warm your house is. I'm cold from sitting to Mr Ward. Sitting produces its own coldness, doesn't it?'

Introductions: I suddenly found myself nervous and stumbling over my words. Roy calm-headed. The topic was the lack of painted portraiture today. Would Graham Sutherland be good to paint the Queen? 'Why not you?' the Queen asked me. Controversial subjects such as Lord Snowdon and his documentary film about old age were avoided; Prince Charles eulogized, and perhaps just a suggestion of criticism for his father sending him to a tough school. 'Now he doesn't need to be toughened any more.'

The Queen applauded the reappearance of the old *Tatler*. I described the attack on its existence by *The Observer*. 'What's this I hear?' asked Jakie, ready to defend the family honour, and conversation became general. Leo spoke the English language in a flowery manner that is seldom used by Englishmen today but which is utterly delightful. The Queen, on hearing a particularly well-planned compliment, said: 'I must remember that.' Now, Diana, Doggie nestling in a shiver at her bosom, with vodka and wine under her belt, did a virtuoso piece on spending the weekend with the 'Horse', Harold Macmillan, and described how Ava Waverley had been '*décommandé*'. The fact that Macmillan was continually referred to as the 'Horse' added to the Queen's enjoyment.

The Queen's car had arrived. It was ignored. Half an hour later the Queen asked Jakie the time. 'I must go!' As the Queen stood in the street, while a few onlookers gawked, I managed to speak out: 'I want to thank you for being always such a support and good friend to me.' The car drove away — smiles, bows, waves…

The party was soon over, for the other guests were late too. But it *had* been a whizz, hadn't it, said Diana.

I have been going through all the old boxes of hoarded letters. The past comes alive with shocking vividness. So many forgotten incidents and discarded love affairs come to light and surprise me.

Some of the letters and documents make me sad; some almost stop the heart beating; the telegram announcing my father's death, the piece of paper with the scribbled words 'out' and 'in' left on the hall table indicating that my brother Reggie was out; he would never come back to write that he was in. A lifetime in a bundle of miscellaneous papers.

DIANA COOPER

Reddish: June 1968

Diana does not wish to pay for a dog's ticket on a train, so it is as well that Doggie is the smallest chihuahua in the world and can be hidden in a basket. Diana, her arm bad from neuralgia, was hugging her leopard-skin bag; no Salisbury porters, of course, but she had no complaints. She has a marvellously Spartan approach to everything. I don't know how she manages to get to all the places she does, under her own steam, no qualms, no anxieties. She appears. Diana is a phenomenon. If she were forty she'd be a remarkable character, but the extra thirty-seven years have only enhanced her strength of personality, her honesty, directness and, to use a word she loathes, integrity. We had a discussion about the word. Gertrude Stein had integrity, but who hasn't? It's an Americanized word; she takes it for granted; those without it are beyond the pale.

From the moment of her arrival, Eileen and I had no chance of a word in edgeways. At seven o'clock I interrupted the flow: 'For a change the sun's come out. Let's go into the garden.'

Diana knows a lot about plants. She knows a lot about everything. She learns all the time and never forgets, so by now she is a mine of information, which is all the more remarkable because she was never educated. But she loves to buy a book in order to learn how to do grafting, or patchwork, or how the digestive tract works, or how broken hips are joined at the socket.

All evening long Diana talked. It was as if she was starved of talk. Yet she has been away among crowds of friends every weekend and her London life is full to the brim. It was pointless to try to stem the conversation, or to interrupt with a query. She just goes on and on. One might as well relax and enjoy to the full the biblical and Shakespearean quotes. And her memory never falters. One cannot believe it, and yet Diana never lies. Diana said she had hated lying to her strict, conventional ambitious mother about her love affairs, her bohemian tendencies; for instance about the hours she spent going round Regent's Park in a taxi necking with Basil Hallam (Gilbert the Filbert). She said it was so wonderful when she married Duff for she never had to lie to her mother again.

I suddenly thought that it was not until I heard Diana on the radio once that I realized how much she has retained of her Victorian-Edwardian upbringing and aristocratic code of manners and speech. 'One wasn't critical at that age.' 'One was too young to criticize.' 'She was lovely, Gaby Deslys; she was splendid, Ethel Levy; she was all that one imagines a Queen of Beauty to be, Mary Curzon.' Diana is a good mimic and can make the face of the person she is describing.

Diana talked of Felix Youssoupoff, and said how she had wanted the great, dazzling beauty to marry her elder sister Marjorie. She told of his kindness to other exiles; how at midnight his flat was invaded by all those who came to lie on the floor for a night's shelter. She told of Jo Widener, who tricked Felix into selling his Rembrandts for a third of their value, and how when in court he ridiculed this 'painted man with high heels'. Diana talked about the horrors of keeping people alive long after they should be dead. 'Can't be bothered,' she said about giving any after-death presents to friends. Diana used to be remaking her will all the time, but now the whole caboodle goes to 'my darling John Julius whose only faults are that he enjoys the pleasures of the flesh'.

We discussed modern art, and where and when it became too difficult to understand. Diana said her taste stopped at early Cézanne and she will not *pretend* to keep up with the times. We talked until midnight about cancer.

It is late, and Diana *will* still delay on the landing, her tactics perfected. She said she slept very little. I did not turn on the burglar alarm as I know she prowls about in the early morning. Recently she inadvertently set off the alarm and the police stampeded into the yard at seven in the morning.

Diana on Sunday was non-stop euphoria in spite of the rain; the Pre-Raphaelite scene down by the river; so many birds; lunch at a friend's house in the next valley complete and utter delight with all the rhododendrons, azaleas and bluebells at Stourhead.

Non-stop talk on the way home, refusing to cease even when the car came to rest in the garage. Talk all evening and late into the night. We were all exhausted, but not Diana.

STOURHEAD

June 14th

The rhododendrons and azaleas were no longer at their best on this second visit to Stourhead. When I went with Diana two weeks ago the crowds on the lakeside looked like personages in an eighteenth-century landscape. The wonderful honey scent of the azaleas was powerful and reminded me of my first heartthrobs at Harrow School. Today there were few people. The calm water and the ever-changing and beautiful compositions of trees were idyllic in the haze of the early morning. It was the sort of day we wait all winter (and spring) to enjoy. The birds seemed to share our ecstasy. In the water the moorhens took off in a dripping euphoria leaving lines of bubbles in the water. The swans were admiring their wings, and the distant shriek of a peacock was not discordant.

Jayne Wrightman's pleasure at the scene was a joy to behold. She is a true lover of beauty in many of its forms. This was a day she had long looked forward to and the whole setting put on a performance of which Hoare would have been proud; the ingenious planting of many variegated trees, the contrasting colours and forms; weeping willows as tall as ilexes, firs as we would expect to see them only in India, maples, the white handkerchief tree; dark mahogany copper beeches; golden oaks, Chinese magnolias of every variety; on the way round the lake wherever one looked a new and equally beautiful picture could be seen.

A horrible summons to New York shatters the peace. I *have* to make a certain amount of money to go on living in the way I do (two houses a great burden). So I *have* to jump at an opportunity to do a big New York production, but as bad luck has it, this always happens in the summer so that the garden I've longed for all winter and spring has to be abandoned, and my tranquillity of mind upset.

Reddish

It is the fledgling season and there are more birds about. The cat, Timothy, has behaved according to his instincts and has had an orgy of slaughter. Ray, washing up by the kitchen sink, is talking to me through the hatch. Suddenly he is silent; he pops his head out of the window; then a minute later says, 'I've seen the most incredible sight! That cat was standing looking up at the yew tree when suddenly he sprang, like a tiger, about eight feet into the air and came down with a young bird in his mouth.'

For as many hours as he wishes, Timothy sleeps on my bed. One day in the garden the Smallpeices complained to me of Timothy's beastliness. He had climbed up the yew trees, upset the too-young-to-fly birds from their nest, and come down with a mouthful of yellow and grey feathers. Corpses of other young birds lay around while bereft mothers flew about hysterically screaming at their tragic loss. Suddenly I loathed the white, decorative cat. How could I allow him on my bed? In a flash all affection for him had vanished.

Many times during the night he returned to scratch and miaow outside my door. But he was not allowed in. I felt the absurdity of my attitude. Perhaps Mrs Smallpeice has the right perspective when she says: 'One cannot blame him, it is his nature; but to see it happen makes one angry.'

A SUNDAY AT REDDISH

June 1968

There was the nice friendly driver from the car hire service to meet me at the airport and drive me to the quiet realm of Broadchalke. Never have I been more pleased to return to my haunts.

Incredible standard roses were growing in the gardens of the ugly villas on the way; every village was a bower of flowers, the meadowsweet lamp-post high. Everything is burgeoning in this marvellous spell of sun and heat. It was the best time of the year and as we drove up I could see the house bedecked with apricot rose fronds. Eileen ran out in a state of euphoria. For two days she had been savouring to the full this peak moment. 'Look!' I was ravished by what I saw. In the interval from last Sunday every rose had come out; it was a plethora. I had never seen so many cushions of pale blossoms. After twenty years, the garden seemed at last to look as I want it to look.

In pleasurable mood I walked round every corner and twist of the garden and gradually the strain of the past week was forgotten. And what a strain it had been! The air trip to and from New York, the delays caused by the 'go slow', the three long conferences to discuss the project on hand, a musical about Chanel.

Then the return to London to cope with chores there before going off to Paris, and the terrible strain of listening to Chanel talk about herself without stopping from 1.30 to 5.30. Never once was I allowed to ask her a straightforward question, so really the exercise was fruitless, except to make 'friendly contact'. But the whole week was a rush against the clock, meetings and dinners, a visit to the osteopath, and the British Embassy Ball; too much to fit in, let alone remember, in such a short time. But miraculously I returned all in one piece (as the Queen says) and able for two days to relax and savour summer.

PRINCESS MARINA

August 1968

When I think of Princess Marina I remember her deep, serious voice, and her sad smile of compassion. I remember her shock at being greeted in the street in Florence where she was never recognized as at home in England, and she was suddenly reminded that she was not just an ordinary private individual. I recall the many photographic sessions in the garden at Coppins with her husband and children, and, at the studio, when she would arrive with a picnic lunch-basket and boxes containing Greek national dress and her formal gown complete with orders and decorations. I can see now the expression of intense concentration as, with dust sheet on the sitting-room floor, she worked with crayons and pencils at her easel. I remember her amusement at Vaynol in North Wales when slowly and ridiculously I fell into a lake fully dressed; and after a dance at her country house when she and her sisters, in nightgowns, laughed with the other house guests about the incidents of the evening.

The arrival in England of the strangely beautiful Princess Marina of Greece to marry our Prince George gave us all an excitement and stimulus that will be hard to forget. Those who had the good fortune to meet her could see the cool classical features in a perfect oval head held high on a straight column of neck, the topaz eyes, the slightly tilted smile, the apricot complexion, and the nut-brown cap of flat silken curls.

She became an adornment to the general scene, and wearing simple Greek draperies, or Eugenie crinolines and romantic hats, her likeness to the young Queen Alexandra was felicitous. We soon knew that she was a character of great gentleness and modesty, with a natural gift for draughtmanship, and a love of music. She enjoyed the company of people with creative talent.

Then one dark wartime night, at a tragically early age, she became a widow; for hours on end she remained speechless and motionless as she stared out of the window. The people grieved with her then as they were to do for the rest of her life.

It was difficult for her to become assimilated into British habits; she had not the knack of making friends easily or quickly, but once she had given her friendship it was a serious and lifelong commitment. Her greatest quality was one of heart. No one had a kindlier or more understanding outlook.

Brought up by her mother with a deep regard for tradition, and steeped in ritual, she was the most simple of human beings, at her happiest in informal surroundings. It was characteristic that, throughout her life, she preferred to serve her friends herself at lunch at Kensington Palace, or better still at an outdoor picnic. Her parties lacked grandeur and possessed a delightful atmosphere of the impromptu, although there was never anything casual or offhand about her. She paid impeccable attention to details. In spite of all that she had to do, she never permitted herself to be hurried or thoughtless.

Her sense of fun sometimes made it difficult for her on official occasions, and she was the first to laugh at herself in some situation which she considered 'och, so stupid!' She loved to give herself up to uncontrollable laughter. Sometimes her amusement was caused by jokes of a quite basic nature.

Beautiful and romantic princesses are a rare phenomenon today, and their mere existence enhances. Even those who saw her only a little were warmed by the knowledge that she was there; with Princess Marina's death that particularly lovely glow has gone from the land.

October 1968

The morning papers all published my new photographs of the Queen wearing a naval boat cloak. As these were quite different from any that I had taken of her before, they caused a stir and were incidentally good publicity for my exhibition at the National Portrait Gallery, a collection of about six hundred of my photographs taken over the last forty years. It has been an amazing success and seems to have been enjoyed by old and young alike.

FRITZI MASSARY

Bühlerhöhe, Baden, Germany: February 2nd, 1969

In the sanatorium, where I had come to recuperate, I had another go at the German newspapers hoping that perhaps, with practice, I might understand a few sentences. By the most extraordinary coincidence, since she was one of the very few German people that I knew, I found myself reading of the death of Fritzi Massary, at the age of eighty-six, in Hollywood: *Fritzi Massary gestorben.*

A pang of pain went through me, for although I had never known her in her prime, I had heard much about her and realized that in the world of operetta she must have been unique. She was the 'Merry Widow' of Germany and very different she must have been from our lovely Lily Elsie. She had a tremendous vivacity and chic. Her clothes were said to be more works of art than theatrical dresses, the petticoats alone worthy of a museum. She was a heroine with an exquisite voice and an impeccable way of putting across a song.

I first met her in the courtyard of Schloss Kammer while staying there with Raimund and Alice von Hofmannsthal. She was a wizened little pixie in Bavarian clothes who sang with great play of fingers the popular 'Joseph' from *Madame Pompadour*. One could tell even under these difficult conditions what artistry she had, and all who saw her were speechless in their admiration. Then, being a Jewess, she had had to flee from Hitler's diabolical regime. In London she had appeared in a Noël Coward musical. In 1963 George Cukor had the idea of casting her as the Queen of Transylvania in the film of *My Fair Lady*. I was given the job of showing her around the lot and taking her to be measured by the wardrobe.

But she was not willing to break her retirement for peanuts. Her agent asked the most preposterous amount of dollars for, at most, a four-day stint. I was deputed to telephone her and reason with her. 'But it'll be fun!' I said very stupidly. 'Fun? No, it will be hard work. It'll upset me a great deal. It'll mean panic here for weeks on end. My peace of mind upset. I've retired. Why should I come and do a day's work if it upsets me?'

She had certainly enjoyed a good life, for although in middle age she had had to leave her country and all behind, she managed to make a new life of ease and comfort with her daughter Lise in California. It would be difficult to explain to later generations the freshness and originality and vitality that she invented, which is a pity; the stars of today could well benefit from her. Maybe a number of older people will be sorry that Fritzi had gone. I blow a kiss to her memory.

That evening I wanted to watch on television a programme in memory of Fritzi Massary. What a joy for me that would have been! Beforehand I had to sit through a performance of *The Glass Menagerie*, and then a political discussion which seemed endless. Just as I was looking forward to what I had been waiting for all evening, the other guests of the sanatorium rose to their feet and one of them turned off the television. In English I shouted: 'I want to see Fritzi Massary!' 'No, no, it is too late; it is forbidden.'

London: Easter 1969

I arranged to take the recently widowed Sybil Cholmondeley to the premiere of the film *Oh What a Lovely War*.

There are few people who still manage to have the aura of pre-1914 luxury about them, but Sybil Cholmondeley is one of them. During winter, she is likely to wear a tuberose pinned by a pear-shaped diamond brooch to her dress. Tonight she provided a marvellous half-bottle of champagne and smoked-salmon sandwiches and, fresh from Norfolk, her keepers had sent three plovers' eggs.

'Now you must do what my brother Philip taught me to do with them. You must redistribute the yolk. Now, my hand is quite clean, open the palm flat, place the egg with the flat base in the centre — now be brave! Bring the other hand down on it very suddenly and hard — slap — like that — the egg suddenly becomes a poached egg, flat and with the yolk seen through a film of white jelly.'

I felt I had had a glimpse of another world — the world I had yearned for as a child.

Of the evening only the film was a disappointment.

Edward Bond's play *Saved* caused a furore when it was first shown only a short time ago. Already it has become a classic. I must say it's outspokenness, frankness, and brutality shocked me. But the shock was legitimate and not for shocking's sake.

I found the play a real development in the art of play writing, subtle and brash at the same time. A young man living with a girl in her parents' house is superseded by another man whom he hears fucking his girl downstairs. He shouts: 'Are you trying for the Cup?'

The mother sympathizes with the rejected young man. 'But how do you manage?' she asks.

The most terrific shock came at the end of one scene after the mother had inadvertently sexually excited the boy, then scorned him in disgust, and the young man gets out a dirty old handkerchief and starts to unbutton his flies...

A later scene, between the resigned, but vindictive husband and this boy, was really wonderfully subtle, sad, poignant and strange. Very impressive ending to thoroughly stimulating evening.

A PLEASANT EVENING

April 1969

The pleasant evening was a quiet dinner at home with Elizabeth Cavendish, Frank Tait, and Patrick Garland. We all got along well and the talk was of a most entertaining quality. Patrick, a new friend, is extremely funny as a raconteur and brilliant as a mimic. But the mimicry is not overdone; he does not do set pieces, but tells his tales in the person concerned's voice. He was full of good stories about *Forty Years On*, and how John Gielgud is so absent-minded that he is often late for cues. He once missed a whole scene and, doing an ad lib, said to the audience what was most in his mind: 'Oh, I'm dreadfully worried about having to pay all those back taxes.'

Another Gielgud story out of context. When they were rehearsing *Oedipus* and the gold phallus was first produced there was much criticism. Irene Worth said: 'It should be on a plinth.' John asked: 'Prince Charles or Prince Philip?'

Patrick also talked of the very shielded Julia Trevelyan Oman, the designer. Her worst ejaculations are 'Oh Christmas' or 'Golly'. During the fighting stages of preparation for *Forty Years On* she heard so much swearing that she asked why everyone said to her, 'Oh, go and fuck up.' However, conversation was by no means all bawdy.

Patrick has a very wide knowledge of poetry, literature, and the stage, and his honesty is remarkable for one going through the beginnings of success. Talk was also of the remarkable village in the south of France and its 'inhabitants' bought by Tony Richardson, and the goings-on, which Elizabeth saw as a guest last weekend; a great deal about juvenile delinquency; Elizabeth, a magistrate, had today sent a child to a reform school for stealing £2,000; about the Budget — we are all having to pay higher costs amid the general gloom of the long, dark, cold winter. Ill-health, Biafra, Czechoslovakia, and all the horrors of the world today.

We went on until one o'clock in the morning which is now a late hour for me.

KENNETH CLARK

Spring 1969

Tonight I saw the last episode of *Civilization* on television. This series has prevented my going out on Friday or Sunday evenings. It has given the greatest possible pleasure. The most exciting of all was 'The Fallacies of Hope', with its miraculous use of music.

It is not surprising that Kenneth has aroused enormous jealousy. He knows too much and he knows that he knows more than others. Yet one cannot but admire him. Though one is alert to criticize, the guarded phrases in which he cloaks his opinions are so exact and clever it is impossible to worst him.

He is fortunate to have had this opportunity to show to a large public the fruits of his life's work.

DAVID HOCKNEY

Reddish: Whitsun 1969

It was the first time that David Hockney came to stay. For three days I have been studying him while he savoured all the impressions of Wiltshire and, monkey-like, squinted or grimaced up at me, then down again to his drawing pad. He has been asked to do a drawing of me for *Vogue* and since I admire his work, I was willing to sit until Domesday if he needed that time to get a good result.

To begin with I was utterly appalled, having remained in some romantic but extremely uncomfortable pose for a great deal too long, when I saw an outline in Indian ink of a bloated, squat, beefy businessman. He laughed. No, it wasn't very good, and he embarked upon another which turned out to be just as bad. About eight horrors were perpetrated while the days advanced until, finally, something rather good emerged. He was encouraged. He was enthusiastic. Would I sit again tomorrow all morning and then again after lunch. He eventually decided to draw me in pencil rather than in ink and the result was different and better.

Poor Roy Strong did not seem to have much attention given to him, and he had recourse to doing watercolours in the conservatory and garden. David, tireless, continued with his drawing with infinite care and precision. I marvelled at him as he sharpened the pencils (having discarded the pen) for the hundredth time. I realized what a very different sort of an artist he is from myself. He has a great technical flair. He knows about cars, he can open unfathomable locks, he knows how to put things together; how paint and pencils work under certain conditions. He is an engineer, but he is also that strange thing, a phenomenal genius.

It is always fascinating to see someone as remote from oneself working in the same field. I was intrigued to see him admiring things that I like from a completely different point of view. We could not be farther apart as human beings and yet I find myself completely at ease with him and stimulated by his enthusiasm. For he has this golden quality of being able to enjoy life.

He is never blasé, never takes anything for granted. Life is a delightful wonderland for him; much of the time he is wreathed in smiles. He laughs aloud at television and radio. He is the best possible audience, though he is by no means simple. He is sophisticated in that he has complete purity. There is nothing pretentious about him; he never says anything he does not mean. In a world of art intrigue he is completely natural.

He was born in Bradford on the day that Michael Duff and I gave our elaborate *fête-champêtre* at Ashcombe. His family were poor and had little interest in art, though David's father surprised the family when years later he saw a reproduction of the Leonardo cartoon which the National Gallery were appealing to buy, and said: 'Oh yes, I've done that; it's called "Light and Shade".' (He had had some art tuition.)

David had three brothers and one sister, and his mother never went for a walk in the country without picking everything she knew to be edible in the hedges. Nettle soup was a great favourite and in a huge, yellow bowl she made very intoxicating nettle beer.

David, inspired by the pictures in the *Children's Encyclopaedia*, knew by the age of ten what he wanted to be. At sixteen he left school determined to be a commercial artist, and he took his portfolio around Leeds with no success.

During his National Service David showed his independence of thought by becoming a conscientious objector. He helped bring in the harvest for Sir Richard Sykes whom he refused to call 'The Master'. He then worked in hospitals, at first in the medical wards where bronchial cases were treated. He saw many people die of heart attacks. He became an orderly in the skin-disease ward. One particular, pot-bellied old man whom he loathed had to be dabbed with calamine lotion. Standing up naked in front of David he would say, 'Don't forget the testicles, David.' David was then given the job of shaving and washing corpses. The thing he disliked most was washing the mortuary floors.

In 1953 he went to the Bradford School of Art. After four years he went on to the Royal College of Art in London. During the first term he finished four drawings. He lived for four months on £30; but in 1961 had saved enough to buy a forty-dollar ticket to New York with a hundred dollars in hand. He lived there for three months and dyed his hair 'champagne ice'.

When I went to the college to take a few lessons, David and his friends were referred to by the professors as 'the naughty boys upstairs'. I visited them up there and found David at work on a huge Typhoo Tea fantasy. Everyone seemed to be doing what they wanted and loving it. The school at this time boasted Allen Jones, Ron Kitaj, Peter Phillips, Derek Boshier, and Pat Caulfield. I bought an indecent picture, 'Homage to Walt Whitman', by David who brought it round when Pelham

Place was in the throes of building alterations. The workmen were startled at his appearance.

David is a meticulous worker, never hurried. He seems to have infinite leisure. He has a great taste for literature, having as a boy got books from the public library. He devours the encyclopaedias and remembers everything he has read.

His Bradford lilt gives a melodic and touching quality to his sentiments. His voice, though low, has a great range of sound. He can touch one's heart with his euphoria. His words are carefully chosen and often unexpected. For instance, he says that someone is 'not immune to the oddity of a situation'.

After dinner at Dickie Buckle's, David talked of the coming of the Golden Age. He had read many philosophers, and has thought a great deal. In the next forty years all will change. The computer will do away with work; *everyone* will be an artist. No need to worry, all the leisure in the world, everything will be beautiful. There will be no private property, or need to own anything. Everyone will be ecstatically happy. It was marvellous to see this white-skinned, champagne-topped, dark-glassed young man in pale pistachio green, with bronze boots, orange and yellow alternate socks, holding forth with such vehemence. Midnight chimed without his realizing that it was bedtime. David goes to sleep only when, suddenly, he is tired, and wakes only when he has slept enough: never a question of routine.

May 10th, 1969

A novella should be written about Anne Tree's governess, Miss Bolton, a bad character, now seventy-five; half Swiss and generally unpleasant she none the less inspires complete devotion, affection and profound love in the heart of Anne. Miss Bolton came late in Anne's youth, at a time when she was still suffering from the effects of a demoniac governess — she does not tell others that this mad woman would come into her bedroom at all times of the night and make menacing faces and gestures. Miss Bolton was not good as an instructress, never helpful in the house, and in fact was hated by other servants. But she seemed to be the only one who was able to give comfort to Anne's father, the Duke of Devonshire, by playing cards with him, when his son was killed in the war. Miss Bolton's selfishness is beyond description and her besetting sin is greed. She eats so much that she now looks like a big, bursting muffin. The doctors tell her that it is a strain on her heart to carry so much flesh, but her podgy hand still goes out to a Bendick chocolate peppermint or another sandwich. She complains everlastingly, is never satisfied or grateful. 'Ha! not much of a tea. I suppose I'll have to go back to my little dungeon hungry for the night.'

Yet I do see her companionable charm. Just to have her sitting deep in a sofa and blinking in front of you is quite a cosy experience. She fills a room with a warmth, more than any dog, and she does not mind having her foibles laughed at. She is the spoilsport of all time. 'Oh, come, do turn off that horrid TV.'

When after fifteen years Anne and Michael had, for financial reasons, to leave Mereworth Castle, they dreaded breaking the news to Lilian Bolton. They approached her tactfully. 'Lilian, we have to cut down. We can't afford it here any more, but I want you to know that, wherever we go, we will take you with us, and have you in the family as always, even if we have to build you a little house in the garden.' Miss Bolton snorted: 'Hmm! I hope it faces south.'

However, the moment came when Miss Bolton could not look after herself any more, so until Michael and Anne found a new house, she must be taken to a sort of old-folks' home run by nuns. 'Nuns, they're some sort of servant, aren't they? Well they'll look after me well.' But the leave-taking was heartrending. Anne hugged her: 'Well, Lilian, we'd better be off, hadn't we?' 'Yes, otherwise I'll be late for lunch.'

Anne, angel that she is, goes down to the home to take out Miss Bolton whenever possible. 'Oh, the happiness of it! We go out and guzzle.' 'We'd better hurry, Anne, or they may be out of "sweet".' She tucks in to pretty revolting food with relish but not gratitude. Anne, loving the companionship, says, 'Oh, the joy, and we'll have her back as soon as we have another home!' Even Michael, who earns a halo for his patience, says he misses the old pig and sends her postcards whenever he has nothing else to do.

Reddish: July 21st, 1969

Unbelievable thrill of watching on television, like six hundred million others, man's first journey to the moon. We could not believe that we were actually watching men up on that bright crescent that could be seen in the sky from the garden on this marvellous summer's night.

Irene Worth, Elizabeth Cavendish and James Pope-Hennessy were staying and we sat glued with pulses throbbing and fears that there might be some last minute, unforeseen disaster. The terror continued. How *could* such courage be?

The whole thing was a great American triumph, marvellous beyond dreams from the scientific point of view. The heroes used poetic and imaginative phrases. Instead of the expected 'say, brother, you should see these colours!' Armstrong said: 'That's one small step for man, but one giant leap for mankind.'

They performed faultlessly their prescribed tasks and answered becomingly the congratulations of the whole world from President Nixon. Before they returned to earth, they left an olive branch and medals in homage to the astronauts who had died in earlier, unsuccessful attempts to reach this fantastic goal.

The household was up at 6 am to watch the splash-down, all but James, suffering terribly from DTS — what a tragedy! — and so vivid was the way that this expedition had eaten into the subconscious that none of us had been able to sleep soundly.

An event that we will never forget and will never be able to understand.

IRELAND

August

It is of great benefit to escape from one's own surroundings. I met Henry McIlhenny at the Russell Hotel in Dublin, in time for prawns and sole at lunch. I felt I was living in the privileged class when the waiter asked Henry if he would like to take the fish off the bone. Henry replied: 'Oh no, you do it — it's too tiring.' Henry laughs a lot. It becomes a habit and sounds false. But Henry is a nice person and fair, and often very kind. He really uses his money imaginatively. Few people know as well as he how to be rich. And he *is* rich. The house in Philadelphia has fantastic pictures and this 1890 castle in Donegal is extreme in its comfort: peat fires scenting every bedroom, full bottles of Floris Lime by the bath; excellent meals. There is a beautifully stocked garden with auratum lilies eight feet high. I understand when others say it looks like a public garden, but it is of infinite interest and tended with extreme care by eight gardeners.

Henry has become very much the host character. His observations punctuated with 'you know' and his voice has acquired an exaggerated sing-song of exclamations that is easy to copy. 'My dear, the price of things! I nearly fainted but I had to order them. Those huge pots come from Florence. They cost nothing! But *nothing*. It's the freight that's the hell of it, and I had to order forty!' Henry gives a thumb-nail sketch of his guests (they pour in for every meal): 'So-and-so's just written a play about Pontius Pilate — such a queer subject my dear. It got rave reviews in Belfast but it never got to Dublin.' 'He's all right, perfectly respectable, with a good-looking wife and nice Rolls-Royce at the door!'

Some of Henry's guests were intolerable. I put up with Americans willingly only when I am on business bent. On holiday they are too trite. One old trout from Charleston was bemoaning the way the world is going. 'There aren't any servants any more, and I'm not going to do my own cooking. I'm not interested, and I hate kitchens! My daughter is a very good cook, but I don't want to go in and watch her preparing dinner, and get a lot of grease in my hair. And there ain't any men left either. American men have no stamina and they all die ten years younger than the women. I hate old women! All women should die at seventy. Then life's becoming unattractive. It was all right until after the last war, but I knew life before the 1914 war and then it was something!'

Moving on to Derek Hill was a great contrast. I had only ever seen pictures of his Vuillard-patterned house. Inside the clutter was of an untidyness and shabbiness unparalleled. The brilliant cobalt-blue walls in the outer hall were peeling and wet. Some of the curtains were hanging in shreds, the china was mixed and chipped; books bulged from the shelves and some were laid horizontally on top of others. Overcrowding took on a new meaning. Pictures like postage stamps on the wall, memorabilia, mottoes, picture postcards mixed up with little original drawings by Degas; among the litter a Corot and a Tonks. The electric light bulbs were too weak for reading purposes. The soap in the bath was almost too small a slither to hold, let alone get a lather from. It was a rather delightful mess and I love Derek for his lack of self-consciousness about it, particularly as he is so over-careful in creating a good impression, in wanting to be loved.

Derek is a sad character and I feel he is deeply disillusioned about life. He never seems excited or exuberant; nothing is quite as good as he thought it would be. He has removed himself quite a way from everybody, though he does have more good and loyal friends than almost anybody I know.

I enjoyed being with him and getting to know his wonderful cook Gracie, but I wish that the sun had greeted us on waking for just one morning during this very cold and damp visit.

Departure from Donegal

It really was the hangman's call. It was dark outside when Derek called me, but I had already heard him banging about and doing his last-minute packing. We had to make this early start to motor to Belfast because there had been stories of motorists stopped and all their baggage and papers carefully examined. As it happened, we were so early that no one was around at the border, and the deserted roads were only inhabited by animals. We had a complete demonstration of nature as we drove through families of magpies, and many more rabbits than one would see in England. Squirrels, mice, rats, hares and stray cats crossed our path. Only the bird life is lacking; the Irish countryside is said to be too poor for many birds to survive.

At Bogside the barricades of burnt-out lorries, trash of all sorts and barbed wire seemed merely fatuous and childish, but I suppose during the recent fighting they were of importance. Now the whole mess merely highlights the stupidity of the Irish fighting one another with the result that all are poorer even than they were before, and life in Ireland today is abysmally meagre. But the Irish love to fight. It is their means of getting rid of adrenalin, and the many issues at stake are so complicated that they are not likely to be cleared up now, or for a very long time to come. Meanwhile life is always uneasy when the IRA are around, and lately their activities have been felt in many sinister ways. Let us hope they will not be vicious enough to resort to their old tricks of destroying beautiful old houses, and setting fire to stables without letting out the horses. We crossed Londonderry bridge guarded by sad, very young-looking soldiers with their guns at the ready. It gave one a pang to see them. It reminded one too much of the last war.

The day was grey and the long wait in the cold air made me very impatient to leave, and to return to less hilly, wide open scenery and to an easier way of life.

Andy Warhol, looking through some art magazines says: 'Isn't the art scene today revolting! Oh I wish I could think of a way of making it worse!'

New York: September 1969

Saturday. All morning spent with Michael Bennett, the choreographer on *Coco*, at his fantastic, eerie, psychedelic cave of an apartment; magenta, scarlet, emerald green with blue spotlights, a favourable and unexpected atmosphere in which to work. If anyone is going to save this show, it is Michael

Bennett. He has worked hard and brilliantly with utterly real and lively conceptions. It is amazing that he does not ever seem to need either food or drink.

I did not mind when he asked me to abandon a whole set of costumes; he was right, for somehow they were wrong. The project, at last, seems to be an exciting one. Such a change; I have all along been *pretending*. So much time wasted, so much energy gone down the drain and sheaves of notes completely outdated; but now I am inspired.

Sunday. A peaceful spell of work in my hotel bedroom, enjoying doing the new designs to replace those that Bennett knew were wrong. By degrees the pressure under which I have been for so long in England (and the nervous colitis too) is subsiding, and I begin to feel very much more leisurely in my attitude.

This is the winter season of pornography. *Oh Calcutta* by Kenneth Tynan has given birth to dozens of other rude and nude shows.

The movies and papers are advertising every sort of sex. Nothing is left unsaid. Where does it go from here?

October 1969

On my way to London Airport I got a great thrill seeing a procession of outriders in white helmets, the cavalcade of motor cars and all the panoply of power that usually goes with the arrival of royalty to our shores. The 'Moon Men' had come to England. In one of those cars were the perfectly nice, ordinary men who had made that incredible journey. I thought of the extraordinary experience it must be for them, having spent ten days in those unreal conditions and now to process through the capitals of the world, cheered and feted wherever they go; and, quite rightly, treated as super-heroes.

It must be very different from anything they have known before! Tonight they are being received by the Queen in the Palace.

VERMONT

October 18th

Sam Green and I took off in a small plane with large oval windows and through them had a really beautiful view of New York State, Connecticut and New Hampshire in their full light and colour. It was perhaps part of the real USA, not the hurried glimpse I get down 55th Street.

The autumn colours are more brilliant than at home, and in the hard, sharp light they created a fantastic Samuel Palmer carpet below; most impressive mixture of colour patches, a lot of rich bluish-green with some yellow interspersed, some scarlet and some orange. The silver birches had shed their yellow leaves and were now ivory skeletons, and like thistledown in the distance.

We arrived, picked up a Hertz car and drove up to the mountains of Vermont. We drank fresh apple cider, bought maple syrup, cookies and apples; and 'arty' clothes from a ninety-year-old woman in a broken-down shack. The trees became more golden in the evening sun, the sky crimson. The dirt roads we travelled seemed to lead nowhere, but somehow we managed to arrive at a nice ski lodge. It had a family atmosphere; everyone friendly, log fires. The presence of Sam was agreeable and sympathetic, and it was nice to have this little doll's building to ourselves. We talked for hours.

Eventually I leapt between the sheets and was asleep within a few seconds.

October 19th

Sun the other side of the cretonne blind and, as a breeze moved it, a glimpse of bright-red leaves outside. It was fine mountain air that came through the window. The sounds of activity outside were all connected with outdoor sports; people going off to hunt birds, and to hike, taking picnic-baskets with them.

It was a welcome change from pressures of the theatre which I had just left behind. Sam drove the rented car brilliantly and we had a long and enjoyable day sightseeing; Putney, Athens, such odd names, which all meant a great deal to Sam who spent his youth here at school so this for him was *le temps perdu*. We walked through yellow and orange avenues of trees, saw the ugly locals dressed in scarlet jackets and woollen caps armed with bows and arrows to shoot deer. It was a medieval sight. We pottered among gravestones, climbed a mountain and, although the skies greyed over, sat and picnicked, the chicken and sandwiches all tasting of the cardboard boxes in which they were packed. Sleepy with sun and air we returned, and I slept more warmly and deeply than I had for months.

New York: November 1st

Bennett's choreography moves me. I am deeply touched by the Parade of Fashions in the finale. But much of the show is banal Broadway fare; the music without distinction and much of the dialogue is anathema to me!

November 9th

Alan Lerner makes me nervous with all his suggestions, some

of which are bang on the mark. The fact that we are opening tonight is terrifying.

Let us only hope Broadway will take to it. The critics will not, of that I'm sure.

November 13th

Jayne Wrightsman was at her best working with her team of experts, fixing lights, deciding the placing of fabulous objects, and making plans for the opening of the Wrightsman Collection Exhibition. By the time I came out of the Museum of Modern Art, my spirits had lifted and I was more pleased with life than I had been before this latest theatrical debacle.

November 14th

Enjoyed a rare walk and even a spontaneous visit to the Frick collection. Here, in tranquillity, I enjoyed the primitives, the Bellini, the Goyas, and a Turner. I realized how my taste had veered away from the French and English eighteenth century which I used particularly to admire.

At lunch Lincoln Kirstein was at his most epigrammatic and devastating, shooting down in flames everything sacred and sacrosanct. He sums up people brilliantly, gets the tone of a person's talent, and is altogether rare. He described the contemporary American painters at the Met. as nothing, absolutely nothing, a fart without a smell. We laughed a lot and our lunch went on to 3:15.

December 8th

I don't quite know why I have such a macabre interest in studying the obituaries in the newspapers, but it gives me a stab to learn that some actress whom I have not seen for forty years has joined the great majority. This morning I was saddened by the deaths of Eric Portman and Hugh Williams, two actors that I have known only a little but who have always been part of the current scene. I suppose the fact that they were both my contemporaries has given me this particular shock and cause for pause.

December 12th

A great dinner, followed by a little dance, given in her white, over-decorated house by Mary Lasker. It was a Democratic Party gala honoured by ex-President and Mrs Johnson. I suppose snobbery and propaganda make one alter one's opinions, but having been revolted by Johnson during the time that his ugly face appeared every morning on the breakfast tray, I now thought him quite passable, and even with a certain charm and gentleness of manner. At the end of dinner he got up to make a speech in honour of Mary. It was done with grace. Naturally he has had a great deal of experience, but it was wonderful to see his mind working as he shut his eyes and decided what he was going to say. He rounded off long and complicated sentences with style.

The evening should have been interesting for there were certainly fascinating people present — doctors, bankers, politicians and journalists. But there was also complete dross, and, unfortunately, the noise was appalling. I soon found myself drained of energy, and beat an early retreat.

Reddish: Christmas Day

Such a wonderful, enchanting view from the top of the Downs looking over towards Fonthill, as I drove out to my Christmas Day lunch with the Trees. It was a sunny day and the winter scene was strangely soft and welcoming in a haze of sweet-pea colours — pale buff, pale mauves, pale blues and rose. It was of simple, basic shapes; the distant woods were bare; a living sculpture.

I realized what solace to the spirit I had been missing while in America. I was pleased with Anne's highly civilized conversation; honest and funny. Anne is one of the best that England produces and I came away deeply satisfied with my happy outing.

In the afternoon I read Enid Bagnold's excellent autobiography. In the book all her qualities are apparent; also her dislikeableness; she is *not* a nice person. But her honesty and strength of character are amazing, and I feel sorry that she should have spent so much time writing so few good plays.

Her descriptions of past events reminded one of the Japanese film *Rashomon* where many different people tell varying versions of the truth. Enid's version of certain events and happenings was not, I felt, the true one. But the book kept me riveted for three days. It is a valuable legacy for her to leave; an important and profound reportage in depth of a strange, remarkable, original and warped life.

PHOTOGRAPHING MAE WEST

January 1970

On arrival in Hollywood at the huge 1920s cement apartment block which Mae West owns, I was surprised to find how small her personal quarters are. To begin with I was fascinated; white carpets, pale yellow walls, white pseudo-French furniture with gold paint, a bower of white flowers, huge 'set' pieces of dogwood, begonias, roses and stocks — all false.

The piano was painted white with eighteenth-century scenes adorning the sides, a naked lady being admired by a monkey as she lay back on draperies and cushions. On the piano was a white, ostrich-feather fan, and heart-shaped, pink rose-adorned boxes of chocolates with nothing inside but the crinkled brown paper. A box of Kleenex was enclosed in a silver-lead box. Lamps were converted from huge Victorian china figures of lovers. There was a great display of photographs of Mae West retouched beyond human likeness all in silver frames. Dust was covering everything. In a nearby lavatory, for instance, a discarded massage table looked grey and it was only when I put my finger on it that I discovered the dark red, artificial leather beneath.

Perhaps Miss West likes to preserve every dollar she has earned. She seems quite contented, or so it appeared from my short glimpse of her during the afternoon photographic session. Miss West's entourage consisted of about eight people from the studio, her own Chinese servant, and her bodyguard, Novak, an ex-muscleman. She was in the bedroom. She had 'finished her eating' and was feeling 'most uncomfortable'. She had put on weight over the holidays and her dresses would not fit. She was rigged up in the highest possible fantasy of taste. The costume of black with white fur was designed to camouflage every silhouette except the armour that constricted her waist and contained her bust. The neck, cheeks and shoulders were hidden beneath a peroxide wig. The muzzle, which was about all one could see of the face, with the pretty capped teeth, was like that of a nice little ape. The eyes, deeply embedded and blacked, were hardly visible. She smiled like an automaton. She gurgled at the compliments. She seemed shy and nice, and sympathetic. When I told her that Lady Sitwell had seen her at a party dressed all in white looking like a vestal virgin, she pretended to be shocked.

She moved very slowly into the living-room and stood — she could not sit — on very high heels. She stroked her yellow fronds of borrowed hair with fat, pointed fingers on which a dozen false diamond rings sparkled: her fingernails grown to several inches in length. She preened and her audience gasped with admiration.

'Oh, Miss West, you have never looked so beautiful — the lighting is so soft.' Miss West chortled.

As a prop, a young Adonis, a former athlete from the local university, Tom Shelleck, had been corralled from the film studio to be included in the photographs; a more outrageous combination could not be imagined, this beautiful, young, spare, clean, honest specimen of American manhood, and the *pourriture* of this old 'madame'.

She has a sense of humour and is able to laugh at herself. I liked her twinkle; and her vulnerability.

When the whole thing was over she started to walk, but teetered and I caught her just in time. By now, the apartment had become too cloying and airless and I escaped.

The most important thing about Mae West is her genuine belief in herself. She is not putting on an act. Lying on her bed and looking up at herself in the ceiling mirror, she says: 'You can see that you are a queen,' and she believes she is a queen.

She looks after herself well, living on health foods, and has become interested in the occult. She says she has extra-sensory perception. She has a few intimate friends who depend on her.

Recently the young generation has discovered her films and she has had a tremendous 'come-back'.

I told her Prince Charles had thought her 'Chick-a-Dee' was the funniest thing he'd ever seen. 'What a pity he saw me with W. C. Fields! I wish he'd seen me in something else. Well, goodbye dear and I hope we meet again.'

San Francisco

It was a drizzly day outside and we decided this would be a good occasion to 'take our trip', my friend on mescalin, me on LSD. Having taken our pills, we hurried out to do provision shopping at the Safewaymarket. Suddenly, everything became more brilliantly coloured; the packages of food became incandescent, the fruits tremendously red, the vegetables electric green, and the cabbages purple. We were in splendid spirits and arrived home to a particularly glowing kitchen. The little sitting-room was a dark cavern.

Now things began to happen! Reality was only there in fits and starts; all was changing and glowing and moving. There was a moment of terror. My companion was unrecognizable, his beard made his face into a square loaf of bread. The fuzz was horrible. I dare not look at myself. I wanted to feel as if my appearance did not exist, but when I did steal a glance, my mother came back with her wild, white hair and long, long nose. My eyes were incredibly blue and my skin all dappled pinks. I felt a bit quivery and shook like a dog coming out of the water, and I sweated. But I gave into the pleasure of it and had no qualms or doubts. My friend was there to guide me and we were completely happy with one another. In a mirror above me was an extraordinary, blowing sea god, a Triton, with full cheeks and huge, curved mouth, blowing the winds away or spouting forth water; a young sea god riding the waves. My friend's complexion had turned dark red, blotched with green-yellow; his eyes dark puce, his tongue almost black.

Then suddenly a very strange hallucination took place when the water god was reborn and I helped him out of the womb. This scene was enacted at great length.

The daylight fading was an indication that five or six hours had passed. By degrees reality was returning but it was not unpleasant. In fact we laughed a lot. Then hunger took control and I have never enjoyed two fried eggs more, nor had coffee ever tasted better. Very soon night was upon us and sleep was deep.

Sunday

No ill-effects. We were relaxed and content. My friend took me to the Methodist Chapel for Sunday morning service. It was a kind of revivalist meeting. The congregation was made up of clean laundered hippies and negroes, mostly young people who came for a pleasant 'work out' and a 'get-together' in a Christian frame of mind.

The place gradually became packed with hundreds standing at the back of the hall and in the aisles. A rock group started to play, everybody sang, the gaiety was contagious and the entire congregation started clapping in rhythm. A psychedelic screen above the altar flashed all kinds of things, a close-up of a girl's tongue on which an acid pill was poised, and the information that Eichmann was still alive. Jesus Christ was referred to as our Director. Songs by Dylan and from *Hair* were sung. The volume of noise became unbearable. For one-and-a-half hours a condition of euphoria was sustained.

We all linked arms and swayed from side to side in a state of jazzed-up emotion; a new religion?

PERU

February 19th, 1970

The train to Machu Picchu rose above Cuzco, then slowly descended among clumps of eucalyptus, a recent addition to the country, pampas, lupins and broom in bloom; the natives on their farms were looking after their herds, running with bundles on their backs, never idle, the women spinning white wool in dark hands. In stature squat and small, they are not beautiful; their faces are plain and open, and I feel they would never be menacing. At station stops, families in mud huts had grown a few button-shaped roses, beneath which ducks and hens struggled in the mud. Life was at its most basic here; a mother would come out of her doorway with breasts hanging out of her cotton blouse and one felt that birth and lust was all very much a part of existence. Mercifully the rich red soil is extremely fertile so that almost everything grows in abundance and the fruit is quite luxurious.

The train seats were harder with each hour and gradually the laughter of the American photographer became irritating. In order not to say the obvious, I became silent. No oil is poured and I am very English and morose, even unfriendly, except to my friends.

The river gorges became deeper and rougher, the brown-coloured water gushing with enormous force. A scene of great wonder!

By now the fertile, craggy landscape had become more Wagnerian, the slopes more precipitous; one marvelled to see cattle grazing at such a height and at such an angle; paths made by the Incas centuries ago could be plainly discerned on these perilous inclines. The jungle had encroached right up to the river bank; orchids, cacti, wild gladioli and all kinds of lush vegetation; a dark green Rousseau world in which it would be easy to get lost or overcome by unknown misfortunes.

On arrival at the base of the mountain we were driven at maniacal speed by a local guide in a truck. The American photographer continued to shriek with laughter but those of us who were on the roof holding on for dear life, and the passengers inside, were terrified and we all complained bitterly:

'We did not come here to be killed.' The road was so precarious that if the truck had skidded we would have been pitchforked thousands of feet down into the Urubamba River.

Machu Picchu was a wonderful spectacle. It was in 1912 that Hiram Bingham, exploring and collecting butterflies, left his guides and came upon this mountain-peak village which even the Spanish conquerors had never found. He discovered a farming community living on the site of an Inca religious centre where there were temples for the worship of the sun, and temples where 'sacred' virgins had been sacrificed, whose remains were unearthed centuries later. It was also thought that there might be gold there.

The whole complex of fortress buildings is of steep terraces built into the green mountainsides and walled with granite. One flight of steps is like a wild oriental Versailles. The day we were there, vast thundery clouds hovered low over the mountains. Some fellow-tourists were adventurous enough to climb the peak of Hyayna Picchu, a half-hour effort in this exhausting climate and quite perilous. I felt tired and conscious that at this height one's energy is severely restricted. None the less we scampered with the guide like mountain goats, took pictures and were duly impressed by the walled-in rooms for storage or worship, the staircases, and roofless or thatched houses.

This is doubtless one of the wonders of the world and I am pleased to have made the effort to see it, but I must confess that it appeared to me no more extraordinary than Christophe's citadel in Haiti.

February 22nd

Off to Puno to see the market, a well-known sight and one that surpasses all expectations. Two tall trees, covered with hanging moss, make the picture, but the dark reds and navy blues of the women's costumes are an essential part.

The road to Puno, along a fertile plain with craggy mountains each side, was of extraordinary beauty, lush with big bushes of broom in flower, and another yellow-flowering bush like an acacia dotted the river bank. This is by far the most beautiful part of the country we have seen and, encouraged, we decided to go on to Ollantaytambo to see the Inca ruins.

The churches en route were shut; but one baroque church in an empty landscape of blue mountains was an exception; a woman carrying a child produced keys to this deserted, wonderfully romantic, somewhat English-Renaissance-looking building with twin castellation decorations, a doorway carved with archaic angels, and donkeys, geese and dogs on the green sward.

BOLIVIA

February

The town of Sucre seemed primitive and crude. On arrival at the tourist hotel our spirits went to the bottom; a new, dirty, untidy, empty hotel; flies thick on the *hors d'oeuvres* already put out on the various dirty tableclothed tables. The vegetable soup was possible but I didn't feel I could eat any of the other dishes without having an upset stomach for a month. Sleep in my revolting bedroom was welcomed.

At the appointed time, Mrs Costa arrived from the Tourist Bureau, an ugly woman with a broad mouth and too many teeth. She had had a hair-do and a manicure and proved an excellent guide, and though one of the new poor, and living a very simple life, seems not sorry for herself.

She took us into the church to see the famous Madonna which is covered with valuable trinkets given by faithful believers; diamonds, emeralds, brooches shaped like dragons and birds of the eighteenth century, thousands of pearls and watches; the result quite moving but hideous.

We visited the cathedral which is Austrian baroque, white marble and with huge gilt altars and pulpits. There are several churches, all gilt and of an exceptional grandeur for the smallness of this town. I was pleased to see a number of old houses with stucco decoration and pretty wrought-iron balconies. The present economy of the country is bad; the rich have been stripped of their wealth, and there is no tourist trade, so life is reduced to a very low level. There are no attractive shops; an old building that should have been an elegant, decorative store sells only spare parts of alarm clocks or odd bits of machinery. The coloured photographic portraits in one shop might have been made in 1890. The poor people look healthier than in La Paz, more open, with nice expressions, friendly to one another and to strangers.

One market was full of the usual Japanese junk, but the people were fascinating, and the women wore trilby hats. Through a dark tunnel, filled with witch doctors and a blind fanatic reciting his prayers in non-stop fervour, there was another market. This was beautiful, with wonderful fresh foodstuffs, vegetables and fruit and grain, in baskets or huge earthenware bowls. There were flowers too, marguerites and tuberoses. We returned to the hotel restaurant for lunch. The soup was only warm water, highly seasoned curry of tripe, very bad potatoes, veal like cement wafers, and the coffee undrinkable. Beer was good and on this we retired, took sleeping pills and shut out the world.

PLAY-GOING

London: 1970

After the desert of Broadway, an added pleasure to my return home was to find that play-going can be such a treat. On three consecutive nights the theatre in London offered me great delights.

The first consisted of the acting, particularly by Irene Worth, and the direction of Albee's *Tiny Alice*; the play I first saw in San Francisco was as remote as ever on this second visit, but David Warner's performance was masterly. He has acquired maturity. He has gained depth and his performance was full of variety and even in such a solemn part, a great deal of humour.

The next play was Donald Howarth's *Three Months Gone*. I have always known him to be a tender and sensitive man of rare talent. It is possible to imagine that now, after several failures, this one — strangely enough, as it is an obscure and curious play — will be a popular success. This play, too, was miraculously acted by Jill Bennett, not a favourite of mine normally, and even more remarkable was the timing, reticence and reality of Diana Dors. However, of all the theatre joys at this time, nothing could compare with the production of *Uncle Vanya*. It was the best version of any Russian play I've ever seen. I have never known such remarkable acting. People behaved and sounded off in ways I've never seen on the stage before and yet the effect was realistic.

The performances of Paul Scofield, Colin Blakely and Anna Calder-Marshall made one feel that actors have seldom before shown us that imaginative, inspired acting is choreographic in its feeling, and musical in the sense that human beings sound differently when under various emotions. At one moment Scofield, embarrassed and harassed at making a half-hearted love declaration, moved his arms in the air like a cat fighting. It was a little gem of observation. Intense in the scene of hysterical exasperation, he did marvellous things with his hands flat upon his bowed head. His voice lost its mechanical strangeness but sounded as if he were thinking and saying things for the first time. I admire and respect him as an actor of integrity and quality. He has none of the coarseness and vulgarity of some actors, and the adulation of the critics, students, and general public alike is absolutely deserved.

Colin Blakely, showing his forestation diagrams, put on the childlike 'explaining' voice. Then when he said, 'You're so beautiful' to Yeliena, it was as if, in his passion, he had invented the words. There has never been a better Sonya than Anna Calder-Marshall's. We suffered with this little gauche creature who had no self-pity. It was a masterpiece of true observation and feeling.

The director had chosen the perfect actors for each part. The nurse was absolutely 'right'; the grandmother of Gwen Frangçon Davies was a powerful presence. To see her with spectacles and ringed fingers reading a book on a sofa was to be spellbound, and when she altered her position on that sofa, the whole play took on new life.

The scenery was just as it should be, almost non-existent yet full of atmosphere. Such enjoyment in the theatre is rare. I felt I would like to see the play every day, to learn a little of what true acting is about.

Reddish

Diana Cooper arrived for the weekend with Doggie hidden under her jacket and though stiff-kneed was able to walk round the garden. She kept up a pretty good running commentary for the lunch guests, and at dinner gave a *va et vient* of brilliance, quoting Donne. After dinner she reminisced about the time before the 1914 war. She talked of the Casati with great sympathy.

Next day Stephen Tennant made a spectacular entrance for lunch having 'rested' all winter; he had not been out of his bed. I saw this extraordinary figure being helped across the hall. He had a long white beard, was incredibly fat, and under layers of coats and jerseys wore a red cotton, bobble-edged tablecloth as a skirt. As George, his chauffeur, assisted him upstairs, it fell round his ankles, much to Stephen's embarrassment. The cloth was being used to cover up the fact that he could not get into his trousers; an enormous gap displayed a pregnant stomach. Once I was accustomed to seeing Stephen as an elderly man, I found the beard gave him nobility and distinction. He looked handsome like St Peter and it did not matter that he had no teeth.

Diana, who knew him but little, met him square on and would take no over-fine phrases — 'Oh, Diana, you are as beautiful as ever!' 'Oh, come off it, Stephen. Don't over egg the pudding. You're hiding a big stomach. You can't do up your flies?'

The two sparked one another off; Stephen reminisced about Pamela Grey (his mother), Margot Tennant, Harry Cust ('My father,' said Diana), Pavlova, Karsavina, Lady de Grey. Talk was so rapid that it was difficult to follow.

At one point Stephen asked Diana to sing some early songs as he knew she never forgot a lyric. This set Diana off on to Gilbert and Sullivan. Stephen lowered the tone by singing, 'If you knew Suzie as I knew Suzie, ooooooh what a girl!' Then Diana told how she, Cynthia Jebb and the Duke of Wellington once motored from London to Marlborough and sang the whole way.

At dinner at Reine Pitman's, Diana continued to be eloquent. She never becomes fuzzy and always remembers names, dates, and quotes. She was very graphic in word and gesture about twice being bound up by burglars.

THE WINDSOR CASTLE BALL

May 1970

Because I was still in hospital after an operation I wondered if I would be prevented from going to the Ball. As it happened I was given permission by the doctors.

It was one of the most beautiful moonlit nights of a wonderful summer. Windsor looked lively at this hour of the evening with crowds coming out of the theatre and the pubs. The castle was floodlit. Little posses of people stood around watching the guests arrive. Policemen and yeoman of the guard were at every point.

Surprisingly informal in a rather cavernous light, the Queen received her guests at the top of a small flight of stairs. As I got nearer I could see the marvellous sheen on the Queen's skin, her teeth, her lips, her hair. She was dressed in white with some sparklets round the neck and her hair a bit stiff. I have never in my life seen such a marvellous regard or such a look of interest and compassion.

I was thrilled.

The silence after 'Good evening' was broken by 'Are you better?' Prince Philip asked: 'What's all this about?' I explained that I had left hospital to come here. He laughed, as much as to say: 'You must be mad' or 'What else is new?' He would have liked to bully me but I moved on. Patrick Plunket told me to go to the long Gothic gallery where the guests were gathering and a buffet stretched the length of one wall. The party was to celebrate the seventieth birthdays of the Queen Mother, the Duke of Gloucester (he's too old to appear), the Duke of Beaufort, and Lord Mountbatten.

Prince and Princess Paul of Yugoslavia were there, and a lot of German royals, and all sorts of young, including several longhaired young men. Ava Waverley looked like a drawing of an old woman by Dürer, her mouth fallen open and her eyes popping. Her hair was like the fluff of a five-day-old chick. Diana Cooper was a *tour-de-force* of aristocratic beauty in white.

The Queen Mother was wearing pale moth-coloured chiffon with pelisses covered with solid sequins, a big pearl and diamond necklace and tiara. Princess Alexandra looked ravishing, long tendril curls, a dark red satin dress and a sheen on her skin; the most adorable of human beings, she exuded beauty. Princess Anne, with wild hair, was fascinated by all she saw and heard. Prince Charles with crab-apple-red cheeks and chin and nose, healthy, full of charm, and intelligent. He asked me if I was still photographing, which gave me a great opportunity to talk about the recent visit to Royal Lodge.

I sat with a neighbour, Mary Pembroke, and the Hopes; was visited by Sybil Cholmondeley, Chiquita Astor and others who pretended that I looked well. I ate a bit of supper and drank two glasses of champagne.

Patrick Plunket then took me to the Charles II rooms to see the new decoration and the pictures which had recently come from Buckingham Palace. Some of the wall coverings are a mistake but in general the improvement is immense.

Patrick has been responsible for doing all the flowers. Instead of the carnation-sweet-pea arrangements, he got the gardeners to grow vast quantities of green zinnias, tobacco plants and alchemilla mollis to fill the golden candelabra on the buffet and to decorate four huge cones. There was a vast edifice of white eremurus, white delphiniums, and white peonies. Patrick had arranged for a whole syringa tree in flower to be cut down and put into a great malachite pot in the supper-room.

The evening was obviously being a success; everyone enjoying themselves and in good mood and the reason was that the election results had returned a great Tory victory. We had been expecting to put up with Wilson and his lot for another five years but quite dramatically all was changed and here was the new leader in person. I didn't see Heath, but he was there and when he appeared, a cheer went up and I was told that he blushed to his collar.

I felt I had better leave before my strength gave out. I had enjoyed myself and the evening for me was more than replete. The return journey seemed to take no time and at the hospital two giggling Irish nurses were waiting by the front door for me. I felt like a prisoner happy to return after his parole outing. I slept better than I have for nights and woke up next day with temperature normal.

June 8th

E. M. Forster died yesterday aged ninety-one. He was a sweet man; gentle, self-effacing, kind, with great moral courage and a determination to fight for what he believed in.

His last novel was written as long ago as the early twenties. Altogether he wrote only five novels and the fact that he is considered one of our greatest writers proves that quality is better than quantity.

A delightful friend, the last time I saw him was two or three years ago when the Italian ambassador and Madame Guidotti gave a gala for his having encouraged an understanding of Italy at a difficult time. He was invited to stay at the Italian Embassy in London and to receive a gold medal at a special lunch in his honour. When he left Cambridge he got into the wrong train; the limousine sent to meet him at the station waited in vain, and he eventually arrived bedraggled and out-of-breath.

I had always liked to think of him still living in his rooms at King's.

Villa Albrizzi, Este: August

The Albrizzi who own this house have long since fallen on hard times. In summer, if lucky, they rent the house to eccentric English people who enjoy its shabbiness.

Diana Phipps, our hostess, has a deceptively offhand efficiency and an aesthetic appreciation of the joys of living simply. She knows how to organize the household and in a vague, casual way, with the help of her Spanish couple from London, everything works. There are seven of us and two children. Diana does the cooking.

She is completely at ease enjoying the villa, and its beautiful, overgrown garden. The carpets are mostly threadbare, there is little matching china, but the proportions of the halls and rooms are noble; the house had been built when comfort on a large scale was understood.

From this delightful place we drive in a curious mixture of motor vehicles; the cook's car, a rented limousine, or the local taxi; over the gravel paths between the beds of drooping sun-tired roses, through the tall, wrought-iron gates to visit neighbouring sights. Once we went by motorboat up the Brenta, to visit the Villa Malcontenta. It was wonderful to watch Diana's enthusiasm for the Palladian design of the house, the furniture, the beautiful china and glass, and everything that Bertie Landsberg had done for the place.

I had never realized how marvellous his work had been. Now I felt sorry that, having once known him well — I had even helped to chip away the paint covering the frescoes here — I had seen less of him since.

To me the absence of noise is one of the great luxuries today. Italy is usually a nightmare of clamour. Every small country town reverberates with the appalling din of motor-engines. Even the most feeble little car lets off a roar that sounds like the approaching hordes from Hell. A motor-bicycle shatters the eardrums of all but the triumphant rider. It is monstrous that this pollution of God's peace should not be curtailed. This and the encroachment of factory buildings and skyscraper blocks of flats has ruined the countryside.

Lorries bigger than any monster ever created by Bosch or Breughel hog the road for miles letting off farts of stinking black smoke. Only the most reckless motor-bicycles dare to overtake them at the corners, and somehow manage to avoid the oncoming car by a whisker.

Diana Cooper is lying on her bed. Her broken leg has hurt her so much that she has had to leave the group. She keeps her bedroom door open so that she can waylay anyone coming up the staircase.

I go in for a chat on my way to bed. She is depressed and may go back to England to see her doctor. What bravery she shows, always pulling her weight, never complaining. Suddenly I felt a brute, that I had secretly judged her for showing off, for not listening, for criticizing the food, for being deaf. Then I realize how unique she is, for she is nearing the eighty mark.

VISIT TO THE DUKE AND DUCHESS OF WINDSOR

September

Went to the house in the beautiful Bois de Boulogne to have tea with the Duchess. On arrival in this rather sprawling, pretentious house full of good and bad, the Duchess appeared at the end of a garden vista, in a crowd of yapping pug dogs. She seems to have suddenly aged, to have become a little old woman. Her figure and legs are as trim as ever, and she is as energetic as she always was, putting servants and things to rights. But Wallis had the sad, haunted eyes of the ill. In hospital they had found she had something wrong with her liver and that condition made her very depressed. When she got up to fetch something, she said: 'Don't look at me. I haven't even had the coiffeur come out to do my hair,' and her hair did appear somewhat straggly. This again gave her a rather pathetic look. She loves rich food and drink but she is now on a strict diet and must not drink any alcohol.

Wallis tottered to a sofa against the light in a small, overcrowded drawing-room. Masses of royal souvenirs, gold boxes, sealing wax, stamps and seals; small pictures, a great array of flowers in obelisk-shaped baskets. These had been sent up from the Mill, which will be sold now the Duke is not able to bend down for his gardening.

We talked as easily as only old friends do. Nothing much except health, mutual friends and the young generation was discussed. Then an even greater shock; amid the barking of the pugs, the Duke of Windsor, in a cedar-rose-coloured velvet golf-suit, appeared. His walk with a stick makes him into an old man. He sat, legs spread, and talked and laughed with greater ease than I have ever known. At last, after all these years, he called me by my Christian name and treated me as one of his old 'cronies'. He has less and less of these; in fact it is difficult for him to find someone to play golf with. There were moments when the Prince of Wales' charm came back, and what a charm it was! I noticed a sort of stutter, a hissing of the speech when he hesitated in mid-sentence. Wallis did not seem unduly worried about this and said: 'Well, you see, we're old! It's awful how many years have gone by and one doesn't have them back!'

We talked of the current trends in clothes, hippies, nudity, pornography, 'filthy' postcards, etc. The thought struck me that had it not been for the sex urges of their youth, these two would not be here together today. But they are a happy couple. They are both apt to talk at once, but their attitudes do not clash and they didn't seem to have any regrets. The Duke still talks of his investiture as Prince of Wales, and asked me to find out where the crown is that he wore at Caernarvon. He got to his feet (with stick) to look out some illustration in a book and talked of the old 'characters' — Fruity, Ali Mackintosh, Freddie Cripps, Eric Dudley.

An hour passed quickly enough, but I felt we were perhaps running out of small talk when I looked at my watch and realized I must leave for an Ionesco play. The leave-taking was lengthy, due to many red herrings on the way. The Duchess leaning forward on tiny legs, looked rather blind, and when an enormous bouquet of white flowers and plants arrived, she did not seem able to see it. She leant myopically towards it and asked, 'What's that? A tuberose? An arum lily?' The man corrected her — 'An auratum' — 'Ah yes, will you tell them how beautifully they have done them.' I watched her try to open the card to see who this incredibly expensive 'tribute' had come from. I'm sure it cost all of £75! 'Who is it from?' asked the Duke. 'Don't be so full of curiosity,' said his wife trying to read without glasses. 'It's from Jane Englehard!' The two old people, very bent, but full of spirit and still both dandies, stood at the door as I went off in Lilianne's smart car. Through the passage of years I had become one of their entourage, an old friend, and the Duke even said to me: 'Well, between these four walls...'

CATHLEEN NESBITT

Cathleen Nesbitt is the most delightful companion. I have always admired her on the stage and considered her a romantic personality. She is beautiful, decorative, and easy about the house. She embellishes the garden and every room she sits in, and her talk is of the best literary quality.

Cathleen shows a rugged sense of reality that no doubt she has learnt in the theatre. She alludes to Willie Maugham as a bastard. She talks freely of the functions of the body. She is clean-living and clean-thinking, but realizes the importance of the sensual passions. Rivals have surpassed her in the theatre; she has no regrets and is not bitter in any way. She is generous, kind and unselfish; and she has an inner contentment.

It is incredible to think that she is eighty-two years old. Her brain is still quick and alert and her ability to quote at great length from poetry and literature is impressive. She is seldom at a loss for a name from her distant past, and can even put a date to a long-forgotten play. She always has a feast of reminiscences about the theatre and is full of good anecdotes about stage celebrities and occasions. Cathleen is also a wonderful audience and throws her head back in raucous laughter.

She is still wonderfully natural. Her face is bright and clean in the moment of waking as others are after hours of preparations.

She leaps out of bed, runs upstairs, and does exercises like a child. Without much money she manages to be delightfully dressed. As Dot Head said, 'She is the perfect example of how to grow old, and proves how wrong it is to make too much effort in the ways of artifice.'

It was only when I was driving her to the station for her return to London (and a diet of cream cheese) that I popped the question of whether she would have married Rupert Brooke. 'Yes, I suppose we would have married if it had not been for the war. You see, I only knew him for three years and during two of those he was in America and that's why there were so many letters. I keep them in a cardboard box and should preserve them more carefully. But, you see, we were both recovering from unrequited love affairs. I had had that girlish crush on Harry Ainley with whom I was appearing on the stage, and he was having an affair with another woman. Anyhow, Rupert was studying for some Naval Reserve course at Dartmouth, and I went down there to see him; sometimes he came to see me when I was touring. We read poetry to one another, I reading Donne to him, and he reading his poems to me. Rupert said he thought he ought to be thinking about making a will, and he supposed we'd better get married. And which would I prefer — to be left his rather small possessions, or the rights to his poems? Then he went on to say he thought perhaps as he had just started a poetry magazine with Lascelles Abercrombie, de la Mare and Gibson, and he would like it to continue, it would perhaps be best to leave the copyrights to the three of them. After Rupert's death Mrs Brooke, his mother, said it was *quite frightening* what a lot of money came in from the poems; that all England was mad about "If I should die think only this of me …", when the other sonnets were far better.'

Cathleen described Rupert's stocky body but graceful, quick movements, the marvellous colouring, the jutting, unclassical nose, and how he had, by dying so young, achieved lasting fame. A young poet dying in a war is always the stuff of legend, but what if he had lived? Would he have developed as a poet? Rupert had wanted more than anything to be a playwright; he had written two plays, but they weren't any good. Would he have become embittered? What would he have looked like today as a man of eighty-four?

I asked Cathleen about Bernard Shaw. She did not know him well, but he had directed the taking of photographs of the production when she played Perdita and he said, 'No, that's the wrong side of your face.' When she told him she would like, for once, to play in comedy, he said, 'No, your jaw is too pronounced. People should have no chins for comedy.' Once, soon after she came over from Ireland and wanted to be an actress, she was invited to lunch with Sir John and Lady Lane. 'I don't know why, because it was all above my station.' She said Shaw should have been present but he was ill. Henry James, however, was well enough to be present. Cathleen wondered what could be the engrossing topic in which Mrs Shaw and James were so intent. She discovered it was entirely about the stomach troubles of Shaw and James.

When Cathleen played 'Mrs Dubedat' she wrote asking Shaw what she should wear; he answered in minute detail about clothes and character. Cathleen again wrote to the now great man when she wanted his permission to do a play of his on radio. Shaw refused. 'They disturb the voice,' he said. 'They made me sound like a bloody Irishman, when everyone knows I haven't a trace of an accent.'

I never came across a woman who has lived so intelligently in such a variety of circumstances and has overcome all the disadvantages, putting them down to part of life's experiences. Perhaps all the sad things that have happened to Cathleen have made her face all the sweeter.

France: September 1970

Birches, lush greens, pale autumn yellows, gold and silver. The farther south the greater our enthusiasm for the rural delights for which we had been looking. They were even more extraordinary that we had imagined in a brilliant blue haze, and a sunlight where nothing moved. We drove through a valley, marvelling in the soft, feathery trees, the palatial roofs of farm buildings, the richness of the quiet animal life, a pastoral poem.

Nor did the Dordogne disappoint, periwinkle blue and gently moving, seen from a mountain height or on the same level, it was a child's idea of what a river should be, bordered with forests in which fairy palaces with blue turrets were sheltered.

Our arrival for a late lunch at our lodging, 'Le Vieux Logis', was a delight, with the hotel guests sitting on a terrace under an awning of scarlet Virginia creeper giving on to an overgrown, effulgent garden which, in turn, gave on to a white-flowered meadow. The food was wonderful and everything we had hoped for. After dark *pâté de foie gras* with really strong-flavoured truffles, I had a stuffed goose's neck with peas. Sam Green contented himself with a salad tasting of the walnut oil with which it was dressed. Later the afternoon sun became softer for our journey to see medieval Sarlat by night; great beauty all along the way, Beynac particularly worth another visit when, from the height of this château, we looked down on to the river.

Domme proved one of the great surprises, a mountain fortress town in which the English were once imprisoned.

We picked walnuts off the ground, fat, oily, delicious. We saw a dozen farms that could be made into romantic houses. But because of the long rainy season, I realize that I would not wish to live in this part of the world. It has been an interesting week with beautiful things to see, and the countryside has not disappointed.

NEW YEAR'S EVE: MOUTON

December 1970

At Mouton where Pauline and Philippe de Rothschild live and grow grapes, they have converted their farm buildings into magnificent rooms furnished with Renaissance sculptures, Venetian chairs, baroque statues, and a marvellous collection of books and modern works of art. Apart from this they have gathered together an extraordinary collection of precious objects, all connected with the grape and the enjoyment of wine: goblets, Roman figures and bottles, Venetian glass, still-life paintings, old silver, and early tapestries representing the processing of wine, all placed and lit with originality.

There are plans for a new façade, a reservoir, a swimming pool, and always additions that are imaginative and a great improvement to the general beauty. It has become a little principality on its own.

Then, suddenly, permission is given to an oil company to build a whole community of factories and oil refineries with all the attendant chimneys and outbuildings. The site chosen is in the centre of one of the greatest vineyards of France. On the horizon of this green-blue sea of vines which dates back to the year 300, there can now be seen, day and night, a vast flame volcanoing from a tall pipe that pierces the sky and belches forth a long plume of black smoke. When the wind is in an easterly direction, the stench is enough to make one wonder if there is not, any minute, to be an explosion. The tragedy of the *Cherry Orchard* has been brought up-to-date, and emphasized a thousand-fold, for these vineyards should be the pride of France and are part of the national heritage. Philippe sits in bed writing a manifesto.

In England we have had enough snow to make everything white. Here everything was covered with a thick hoar frost. The visual result was quite different, and extraordinarily beautiful. The patchwork of fields was all either pale pea-green in colour or pale greys or buffs. The rivers were a deeper biscuit, while the trees were little puffs of off-whites, greenish, greyish. It was quite unforgettable, and when I was being driven through the country roads to Mouton, the effect of the hoar frost on the tall grasses, the bracken, the oaks, poplars, and pines was of unending contrasts of lace-work.

The bluish mist was dispersing, and a pale sun appeared to light up the trees which were all the whiter against the dove-grey sky. The vineyards stretching for miles looked like cemeteries from the 1914 war.

Lunch would be at 2.30 pm — Pauline would not appear until dinner at 9.30 pm. Meanwhile a beautiful, mysterious walk in the pearl-white misty world with the twigs of trees furred, and the ivy leaves edged with crystal. Philippe dressed as a Boyar, threw bread to the ducks in their new domain carved out of a marshland, and then we returned to a table set with papyrus, pine, and every sort of grass by the home florist and her assistant. *Moules* cooked in rice, commice pears in syrup (orange liqueur) with almonds and the rind of oranges. Then a long awaited, wonderfully luxuriant afternoon sleep.

The weather by now had worsened. Reports of more snow and disaster and avalanches along the Rhône. Mountélimar cut off. Most of the guests had been here since before Christmas and seemed to know the technique of daily life.

Having lain in the dark, unable to move, the moment came when I should turn on the lights. In the mirror over the washstand I stared at myself. Generally I pay as little attention to my reflection as possible. There are very few places where I can see myself in my bedroom, either in the country or in London.

Suddenly I found myself staring at this extraordinary apparition that did not move within the frame of the looking-glass. I was really an alarming sight — wild white hair on end, most of the pate quite bald; chins sagging with a scraggly, tissued neck; pale weak eyes without their former warmth. But this could not be me! It was certainly me at my worst, with the light coming from the 'wrong' direction. I turned — that was better; as good as we can hope for. I stood scrutinizing myself carefully. The upper lip has become longer. The mouth a thin, bitter line. The eyes tragic, old and wild, and of a great sadness. Were there no redeeming features? No. Even my complexion has suddenly become covered with large brown spots, toadlike freckles that were not there six months ago! Surely those on my forehead had appeared only in the last week? I stood in a trance of horror. How could I make the effort to dress myself up in picturesque clothes and try to be attractive to a group of highly critical people? And yet that is just what I had to do.

Pauline has the oriental genius for elimination and simplification. She does not clutter her life, and here, since her illness, she seems to have made it even more full of interests while remaining aloof from so much. She seems to have less interest in self-adornment, and just as at one period in her life, when she had the same wonderful chicken dish for dinner every night of a New York winter, now day after day she wears only a succession of dark jackets with tight, Indian man's trousers in beige of leather or voile. It is a perfect uniform. She has no need for or interest in ringing the changes.

The room where we dine is sometimes the grand salon; it may be the library, or across the Roangi raked gravel path at Petit Mouton. The huge, long-stemmed carafes with the napkins tied round their necks have been prepared by the chief of the 'cave' and are served with interest and deference by Dupont, the butler. Philippe with great ebullience calls everybody's attention to a certain wine. There is plenty of good talk. Monroe Wheeler is a fount of information. Would one call him a busybody? Yes, if he weren't so essentially a kindly character. Glenway Westcott never forgets a name, and knows everything that has happened in the literary world in America for the last fifty years: Stephen Spender is roughly the equivalent in England. Raymond Mortimer is quiet and wise, and is his best, as most of us are, when talking *à deux* without fear of interruption. Francis Watson is a delight, particularly when telling some narrative that is full of shocks and surprises. Two Frenchmen are highly civilized, extremely well-read and informed on all matters of contemporary interest, as indeed they should be being publisher and editor.

Replete with wine, talk, and cigar smoke, I come to my fine linen cocoon of a bed with the knowledge that I am going to have no difficulty in sleeping throughout the long hours, though I cannot expect that the sleep will not be full of interesting dreams. Sometimes I am returning to certain situations that I do not enjoy in life. I am trying hard to empty a tiny attic and staircase with all the litter which gives one claustrophobia. Friends and helpers are not enough to clear away the horrific accumulations. Or I dream regretfully of not having been appreciative enough of Juliet Duff and her good taste. I dream, as does Stephen Spender, a lot of Peter Watson who it seems has haunted more people than most of his generation. Then comes that sensation when one does not quite know if one is dreaming or merely directing one's thoughts along certain channels in which one wants to go. This is very pleasant.

Part VI: South American Idyll, 1971

BRAZIL

The Carnival at Rio: February 21st

Grey skies, heavy heat. The chauffeur an hour late. My upset stomach not improved, a bad beginning to the day; but I was happy to have the company of Julio Senna. The carnival processions started in the early afternoon, and from a stand where workmen were still banging and sawing, we had difficulty in finding our places. Thousands of dancers, old and young, sauntered their way down the main thoroughfare wearing red and white dresses of all descriptions. There was no knowing why they were dressed as Creoles, or Carmen Mirandas, or Louis XIV courtiers. Music was relayed from dozens of loudspeakers.

Suddenly in one group a particular dancer was stricken with an attack of sheer madness and improvised a little marvel of energetic frenzy, eyes lost to the world as his feet became stars. A huge old lady wobbled in a dozen layers of fat. These 'schools' of Samba have assembled from many different neighbourhoods throughout the country, and after preparations that have absorbed them for most of the year, have made their way, many of them from long distances, to the main arteries of the city. Strenuous dancing lasts for many hours over several days. Feelings of theatrical rivalry are very strong. Everyone is a vedette in his or her own light, and sometimes the jealousies burst out in terrific anger. A year ago a man in one of the 'schools' murdered a rival. Some friends of the deceased threatened their revenge. He would be shot at the

156

time of the next carnival. Sure enough yesterday, while he was putting out all the shoes to be worn in his 'school', and mindless of the warning, he was shot dead. The body was buried and the show went on.

The social significance of the festivities is quite remarkable. People who are normally poor, who work terribly hard all the year round and have very little to spend will afford money and time to make extremely elaborate costumes that are in themselves the symbol of riches. Cooks, household-servants, nurses, waiters, dress themselves up as princes, princesses, kings and queens.

The Portuguese patron of a small restaurant, where my host, Walter Moreira Salles, eats, takes part in the carnival every year. He is now over seventy, extremely tall and heavily built; a man with children and grandchildren. Ever since he first came to this country, aged seventeen, he has found the costumes of the Bahian women very beautiful, so every year he goes as a Bahian woman and dances for four days.

Everyone was happy. Everyone had forgotten their cares. They were being applauded by a great, anonymous public as if they were football stars or movie idols. Thin and fat, short and tall, beautiful and ugly, hare-lipped, squinting, young and old they were all giving everything they had to give; that extra reach of the voice, the little stretch more of the hips, the twinkling of the toes. It was exciting to see so many people having the time of their lives without inhibition. Euphoria ruled the day. Huge fat mamas were parading in silver crinolines; even fatter men wearing trains many yards long, holding hands, sceptres, and waving flags. There were Picasso harlequins and clowns in pink and viridian, and flower girls carrying baskets of violets. Everything was imaginative, spangled, glittering, shining bright; in a tradition that has been evolved over the years.

Thousands and thousands of dancers passed through the streets, and the music and drums brought the procession to a climax of frenzy. Suddenly the grey skies opened; there had been no rain for six weeks, although it was supposed to be the rainy season, but now it came down in torrents. In a moment the streets were flooded and visibility was nil.

ARGENTINA

Buenos Aires: February 26th

Never before has Miguel Carcano appeared more elegant, more charming-looking in appearance, so witty, amused and amusing than this evening. He is over eighty years old, but seems absolutely in his prime. He has the grand manner and charm that is seldom seen now; in all respects a gentleman who is shocked if others are not gentlemen too. Miguel took the evening in his stride. He introduced us to the leading members of this very rich club which, burnt by Peron in an effort to destroy the flower of Argentine aristocracy, has now been rebuilt at a cost of so many millions that even Miguel was shocked at the unnecessary extravagance. They pointlessly bought a Thomas Lawrence of the Duke of Wellington, and a marble bath.

February 27th

The next morning we left for Cordoba to stay at the Carcano ranch in the mountains. Journey done with consummate ease and style. A most happy arrival; a huge station-wagon stacked with provisions to meet us. After the heat of the coast, the air felt particularly fresh, even nippy and the scenery was much less tropical; trees that looked like olives but were not; almonds, poplars and local small-leafed plane trees.

One was greeted by the lovely sight of apple trees, thick with fruit, growing in long, silvery green grass, and interspersed with fronds of three-foot-long silver pampas grass through which the sun created flashes of light as they bowed in the breeze; scarlet zinnias growing wild. Three green parrots squawked and flew into the branches above. We circled the mountainside and then saw, beautifully placed in a sheltered valley, 'San Miguel', the stone *estancia* that the Carcanos built for themselves forty years ago. The sun cast long shadows over green stretches from the trees planted by Stella and Miguel early on.

A number of bay-coloured whippets greeted us on arrival at the grey stone steps above the front door through which, a few moments later, Stella appeared, her hands covering her mouth, laughing and crying, 'It is a miracle! a miracle!' I was touched and happy. We kissed fervently, and I saw that although she had become old, she had all the charm, authority, and character of before. Stella has had a wonderful life, full of adventure and experience. Born of an important and no doubt rich Argentinian family, she has benefited by the success, so well warranted, of her delightful and brilliant husband. Apart from everything else, they have a gift for friendship and are much loved by many close friends throughout the world.

Their social success started in the days of Edward, Prince of Wales, when he came to the Argentine. When a fanatic ran up to him on the golf course shouting, '*Viva el Principe democratico!*' His Royal Highness was very pleased.

It was when they came to represent their country officially during the war that I got to know them. I was moved when, on the eve of my departure for the Middle East, they gave a lunch party for me (Georgia and Sachie Sitwell were there, I remember) and they wished me *bon voyage* in champagne (then a rare drink). Here was Stella, seemingly a little smaller, her hair sand-coloured, her skin freckled and a bit wrinkled. But the dark eyes were as full of life and change of mood as ever. It is a fascinating face, for it is the embodiment of all her thoughts; it shows exactly how amused or surprised, hurt or astonished, she is.

Leaning slightly forward, in the way that older people do, she took me to see the Arcadian view from her garden. Nothing could be more lovely in this clear mountain sunlight. There were riders on horseback, and groups of children picking the harvest of dull red apples. She showed me her extraordinary rock-garden and took me to the wooded copses where there were two or three different streams; I loved the effect of the sun in patches lighting ragged clumps of tall yellow daisies and of hydrangeas of all colours. Then a tour of the house, just what I had hoped for. A wonderful shabbiness pervaded everything. There was no attempt at spruceness. Carpets were allowed to become threadbare, and yet there was very beautiful silver in the panelled dining-room; English and French furniture in the bedrooms, splendid equestrian pictures, and Chinese glass decorations on the walls. The corridors are panelled in a local variety of mahogany or covered in light cottons of Paisley designs; brilliant linens in small bedrooms for beds and walls alike; rows of Victorian ornaments, collections of local grasses in a display of glass bottles; lots of books, albums, snapshots of the family, chairs for the whippets, vast arrangements of flowers. But of all the many crammed-full rooms, the most delightful is Miguel's library/sitting/work room: gabled ceiling sprouting from high bookshelves, and a vast elegant ladder at hand to scale the greatest heights. The available wall space and the ceiling are upholstered in a huge Philippe de Lascelle design, done, not in silk, but in cream and dark crimson chintz, in which huge raspberries and paeonies play a dramatic part.

It is really a rare and wonderful room and it makes one smile with contentment. It is here that Miguel writes his histories that have given him such a distinguished position in the literature of his country.

February 28th

Slept so deeply that it was almost like having to switch off a very powerful machine before surfacing. It was very late when I was able to obey instructions to ring twice and wait for an original and delightful breakfast; yoghourt like junket, honey, a dark red apple. Everyone complaining about the unaccustomed cold. There had been a frost in the night! This for midsummer is extraordinary! However, we made our way to the river, to the longed-for bathe in the cascades. It *was* cold, but I was brought up to face Sheringham in August and this was warm by comparison and beautiful in the extreme.

The water rushing from the high mountains is said to possess radium heat and is very beneficial to the health. The currents were so strong that at times it was difficult to stand, but if it could be managed one was massaged all over by the force of the water.

Stella was outspoken, appreciative, kind, with a marvellous memory for the amusing things that have happened to her in her varied career; Miguel so utterly persuasive, repeating one's word if it amused him, and using it in his own sentence and chuckling.

Finding among the rocks a variety of different ferns, he suddenly discovers a wild verbena of a tremendously brilliant scarlet. 'Look at the colour — what *colour*! Colour!' His sympathy and empathy are not at all feigned.

We continued to lie on the huge slabs of sun-warmed grey rock while the gushing torrents gave one a feeling of relaxation and serenity. Appetites were good for an excellent and unusual lunch. A long siesta, then a late appearance at the family tea-table.

Returned from the rocks to find the Martinez de Hoz party had already arrived for lunch. The long-awaited moment when I should set eyes on this great beauty again after five years was at hand. After the initial shock, I realized that her allure and charm and natural gaiety were undiminished.

Here she was in her new guise, with the delicate hands of a peasant who does weaving or sculpting with clay; the eyes wistful and questing; the voice deep and the laugh full of bubble and fun; the legs shapely but surprisingly solid. Before the war, Madame de Hoz was universally acclaimed; crowds at the races cheered her as she made her way to the paddock. Once Bébé Bérard, on seeing her arrive at a ball, rushed up and kissed the hem of her gown!

It is an interesting story: the fabulously beautiful girl who married Senor Martinez de Hoz, an important horse-breeder, and became the best-dressed woman in Paris. Dulce de Hoz's jewels were so heavy and numerous that during the war when the two escaped via Biarritz, the Germans thought they were carrying the contents of Van Clef, arrested them and confiscated the jewels. Miguel Carcano, who was his country's ambassador to France, got them out and made such a fuss that the German ambassador in Buenos Aires arranged for the jewels to be given back. The Carcanos even got compensation for their marvellous racehorses which the Germans had eaten.

In fact the Carcanos played a great part in the subsequent lives of their friends, for it was after staying with them in Biarritz that Dulce de Hoz and her husband came to stay at San Miguel and from here decided to build and settle on a neighbouring mountain.

March 1st

Stella has not been a diplomat's wife for nothing. She can come out with some very strong and unpopular opinions. I love her dearly and am thrilled to have had this remarkable couple come back into my life.

We looked at scrap albums; pictures of the highest life in London, shooting at Dunrobin and Drumlanrig; pictures from India, Bangkok, the Dolomites, Venice, *all* over the world.

It was midnight and Miguel said how much he had enjoyed my helping him to revive the past and to remember so many forgotten friends. With the sad knowledge that I must leave on the morrow, I came to bed.

This had been the high spot of my journey. I have loved being in a very simple but highly cultivated home with such an enlightened, wise elderly-young couple.

March 2nd

The car came to take me to Las Barrancas, the home of the de Hoz's. The rough ride through the mountains was a liver-shaker, and as we drove in circles ever higher we came into the clouds and could only intermittently see the huge, pine-planted terrain created by Dulce and Eduardo Martinez de Hoz. They have sliced off the top of a mountain in order to place their house on a plateau, and for twenty-five years have been creating a fantastic abode far from all the irritations of present-day civilization.

Eduardo de Hoz also has a huge ranch not far from a fashionable seaside place, but they both prefer their mountain fortress.

Duke's huge, childlike, sad eyes greeted me at the door. It was a poor day, no sun; one would see nothing and she had hoped we would go for a ride on horse-back. 'But come, let's have tea.' Dulce looked marvellous in her riding clothes with a heavenly blue stock. She was a most alluring châtelaine and her husband wreathed in smiles of love. Later the sun streaked through the clouds and we set off, four of us, on horses, with two gauchos, one in front and one behind, both dressed in black with large black plate hats. We made a long tour of the property, the horses trained to go up and down the rocky mountainside with never a false step.

Dulce, as I was now able to call her (I was Beaton to begin with) looked like a nineteen-year-old girl wearing a broad little mushroom of a hat tied under the chin. She gesticulated violently with a long simple gloved hand. She is an excellent horsewoman and adores going out to see every aspect of their domain. We returned tired but tingling with health for a rest before dinner at which the conversation was mostly about the Peron regime. Food beyond criticism, cold consommé, local salmon trout, chicken in herbs, a marron soufflé with raspberry sauce. Dulce wore a Grès dress of bright rose red, green and purple which emphasized her innate grace of movement. In French on the ceiling of the salon is the inscription: *Soyez vous-même* (Be yourself). The court around her adore her for being herself as she talks to them in a rather deep, gruff voice. I have become quite enamoured of her. We looked at excellent slides, taken by Eduardo of the mountain as it was before building started and the various phases of the last twenty-five years.

'And now we all go to bed,' Dulce said. 'It is lots of sleep that keep you in such excellent health, shape and spirits.'

RETURN TO RIO

March 7th

I hated arriving at Rio and discovering I was to stay at the Copacabana Hotel, because the Moreira Salles' home was still uninhabitable. It was a relief, however, to find that I was no longer in the same rooms and that the things I had left behind had been put out in an orderly way in the new surroundings. Roses and little cakes and wine were there to welcome me, but there is something horrible about this hotel.

Coming back to Rio I realized some of the differences between Argentina and Brazil. The latter country has no elegant buildings, no culture, the future is everything. The Argentine has not developed since the Peron era, but none the less life is more agreeable. There are less poor, the food is excellent, particularly Argentine beef. Here in Rio, Elizinha says, with no regrets, 'There are no restaurants.' In fact 'no regrets' is a typically Brazilian attitude.

Copacabana Hotel swimming pool

How is it that, hating the rich as much as I do, I find myself in a dump like this? One's eyes never rest on anything beautiful. One's mind never has an intelligent thought; all is dross, and expensive beyond belief I am sure. I spend much time closing my eyes to the horrors of the people who live here and do all the things I dislike.

During the winter in England I said how much I wanted warm sun on my shoulders. I got a bit of it this morning, but at what a price! Screaming kids disobeying their 'Babas'; Americans, raucous Brazilians, all smoking, drinking, covering themselves with oil, not one beauty in sight. I come up to my room longing to read, but I dare not for fear of headaches. This is a bad phase which I trust will pass; never for many years have I felt that time passes so slowly.

March 9th

Walter Moreira Salles had told me that our proposed air trip could be done in one day: impossible, at least in this heat. At last we arrived in the pretty eighteenth-century town of Ouro Preto, looking Bavarian with baroque churches and elaborate façades; rows of houses. I thought it expedient to do some sightseeing before we broke for lunch. It was a joy to see so much that was pretty and picturesque, and worth the effort of the journey. But walking up and down these cobblestone streets in the midday sun was very exhausting, and after three-quarters of an hour, I was sweating and worn out. We ate excellent chicken on a terrace overlooking cedar-coloured, tiled roofs on which vultures were sitting surfeited with their morning meals of dead animals.

More sightseeing, St Francis' church, very late in period, but placed in a dominant and imposing position against the stormy sky, a baroque church of bright gold on gold, the sort of thing that one sees in Spain, Mexico, Bolivia, but this one in mint condition. Fountains, senate houses, ornate windows, beautiful, massive Spanish doors of bold mouldings; colleges, museums, all of a piece.

We drove on through the mountains to another eighteenth-century town, Marianna, where many illustrious poets and artists lived and the march composer Souza was born. The menacing clouds turned to rain and we just made it into the museum before a deluge started that continued for the rest of the day.

The Hotel Rey in Bello Horizonte was modern and congenial. There was a magical effect when two small, coloured pages showed me my room and as if carefully rehearsed, pushed aside a series of light aluminium shutters, then slid back the windows on to a night filled with the lights of the town. A fish dinner in my room, and early night in preparation for another strenuous day tomorrow.

March 10th

In the distance the hill town of Congonhas has reminded us of Italy. It is dominated by the white church with twin towers remarkable for its very fine carving, done in the eighteenth century by a cripple. This man also fashioned the statues on the church, and despite his physical handicaps and difficulties had managed to achieve something that is vibrant and magical and a great wonder. The skies tortured with wisps of cloud intensified the grey of the statues and the simple embellishment of the church.

March 11th

Elizinha Salles said the political situation was much better; that the economy had improved fantastically under the present government, but that there was a very dangerous group of young rebels who were being incited by older men to create publicity and havoc. It was necessary for them to have guards everywhere outside the house, wherever Walter went, and the children were here in the patio playing a game of croquet with the bodyguard.

Elizinha invited me to see their newly decorated house and the garden. A lot of their pictures and furniture had come originally from churches. She explained that most Brazilians could only buy their furniture from Sears and Roebuck catalogues and therefore owned nothing good. I was very impressed by her carpets and some of the jacaranda wood carved by the Portuguese in the manner of Chippendale; a lot of blue and white Lowestoft china came from Macao.

Part VII: Farewell to Old Friends, 1971-4

Reddish: April 1971

This Good Friday was as cold, raw, windy, wintry and bleak as it is possible to be. Nothing to do but stay indoors. Fortunately for me Alan Tagg was staying, and we took the opportunity to change the furniture and effects in the dining-room, winter-garden, and other rooms. Alan has a wonderful eye and sees things that are no longer valid and that I, through living with them daily, miss.

Easter Saturday brought out the sun, and people's spirits were revived. Alan went for a walk before breakfast, and the day was spent out-of-doors discussing with Smallpeice the construction of a lake — of all things — across the road which David Offley says he can fashion for us. Then, at Alan's suggestion, we went for a walk 'to see the village', the cottage gardens, and the spring that bubbles so clearly and coldly to the watercress beds. Faces at windows were as interested in us as we were in them.

The wintry sun was now at the end of a long span of light. We watched a beautiful barn owl, dove-biscuit coloured with a huge wing-span; it flew along the valley, flittered, soared, prospected, then landed; it walked, it rested, then was on the wing again. We saw a rabbit hurrying over a steep hill to safety.

Alan's quick-as-a-flash eye discovered some blue flowers that were rare, with dotted leaves.

EDITH EVANS

May 27th

I was full of expectancy when, after an idyllic sunlit drive through masses of white May blossom, we arrived at the theatre in Chichester.

It is odd how one can tell from a distance if something is out-of-the-ordinary; if there is some crisis. We noticed a huge olive-green Rolls-Royce full of women. Over one of them in the back seat the chauffeur was bending solicitously as if pampering a child or an old invalid. The profile was familiar: surely it was Edith Evans! Was she being told to hurry and get into her dressing-room? Wasn't she cutting it fine? Surely she would prepare for her performance long before this? A rather 'hippy'-looking fan stood by the open door of the motor waiting perhaps to ask her if she would oblige with an autograph. But very slowly, as if in a funeral procession, the Rolls moved off.

I was very baffled. It must be too late for her to be driving away from the theatre? We went into the dark, dreary theatre, looked at Alan's set and were given a programme, out of which fell a slip saying that owing to the indisposition of Dame Edith Evans the part of Charlotte would be taken by her understudy.

The play disappointed. There was much to criticize about the direction, but really the whole evening was ruined by the absence of Dame Edith. Glamour had gone, star quality was missed, and her understudy had none of Edith's charm or wit. I closed my eyes and could imagine exactly how Edith would play the part, how she would get her laughs and give it pith.

Anna Calder-Marshall in the interval told me that Edith had had a nervous '*crise*' at the thought of facing an audience. The weekend had been for her a long time away from the stage. She was only happy if acting continuously. Sundays were a trial. By Monday evening she had worked herself up to such a pitch of nerves that a doctor had been summoned and in her dressing-room had told her that she should not go on. She had been rather odd at rehearsals. She hates first nights; the telegrams, flowers, messages, excitement. The management kept from her when the first night was to be. On the morning of the opening, her chauffeur had telephoned the theatre to say that Dame Edith had not ordered him for the evening. Was she not wanted at the theatre? 'Yes, of course! How important that you enquired, but don't let her know it is a first night.' Edith had — according to Eileen who had seen the first performance with Alan — appeared very tense, but the audience had applauded her every word. It had been a personal triumph, probably her last. What we had witnessed quite by chance outside the theatre this evening was poor Edith's final exit from the stage.[10] She is eighty-three, is wobbly on her feet and getting a bit deaf. At rehearsals she is apt to forget her lines and in order to 'cover up' will invent some excuse for an interruption. 'What is this circular cushion doing here? It's nothing but a designer's peccadillo!' Then she will ask the prompter, 'Where was I?' and, given the missing words, will continue. Although she is still able to play bits in films and television, it is the end of a long and wonderfully productive theatre career.

Gladys Cooper, who is a year or so older than Edith, was unsympathetic when she heard what had happened. 'Her trouble is that she thinks too much about the theatre. She should go out and forget it, but she's so ingrained and self-centred, she has no interests except her performance. I have

---

[10] Dame Edith did, in fact, appear again on the stage after this, giving readings.

my grandchildren and all sorts of other interests to keep me going, and I don't think about my part once I'm out of the theatre. I don't think about myself at all if I can help it. A young man rang me up for an interview on "The Psychology of Acting". I said I didn't know anything about it. I was too busy housekeeping and living my life; and as far as the theatre is concerned, I feel jolly lucky that I've got a good job.' Gladys has always been a realist. She has never treated the theatre too seriously and this has stood her in good stead.

Reddish: May 30th

A big change has been brought about by a huge prehistoric mechanical digger which has bitten into the soggy marshland at the bottom of the field opposite the front door, and has created a lake with an island all for my very own benefit.

It is extraordinarily exciting to see, at night, from my bedroom window the remnants of the light in the sky reflected in the winding ribbon of water. It brings a whole new interest to life here, the element of water.

Even in the appallingly muddy condition with which the landscape is at the moment disfigured, I can tell that this will be a lovely place to look at, with fish and all sorts of birds that are different from those on the terrace of the house. Already there are moorhens, ducks have visited and swans have been seen. As for the trout, it seems I could spend my old age being a fisherman. King Charles said these were the best trout in England.

The house itself is now seen proudly standing in a paved forecourt. Instead of a gravel path of uneven design, we have a very formal slice of green lawn with paving-stones coming to the edge of the box and the yews. It is a great improvement and is a delight not only to me but to passers-by. All that is needed now is some herb growing between the cracks of the stones and things like white foxgloves and valerian sprawling in clumps at the edges of the drive and steps.

Italy: June

A visit to where D'Annunzio lived was interesting; a whole complex of buildings, theatre, lecture hall, mausoleum, colonnades, arches, terraces, stairways, and not particularly inspiring gardens. The house where he actually worked beggars all description. To begin with, it was so dark, except for one room — the study — that one could hardly grope one's way about. Through the gloom things looked fantastic and macabre; gold and black; oriental mixed with Florentine Renaissance and Victorian Danteism; dolls, Chinese figures, badly gilded plaster-casts, plaster-casts trimmed with jewels and draped with gold lame. It could be the eyrie of a black magician, or the heart's desire of a raging faggot.

There were rows of encyclopaedias, thousands of books marked with his tags, chairs for reading and study at every point. He had enjoyed buying useless objects and would perhaps acquire forty pieces of junk all at one go. Because he was a small man, all the doorways were low and the rooms were small.

The airlessness, the slightly dusty veneer, and the smell of mothballs produced a sort of pain in the chest. After two hours photographing, I felt utterly and totally exhausted. I am not generally sensitive to vibrations and atmosphere, but this I felt was really rather evil. I cannot think why a film has not been made about D'Annunzio.

The whole place is now carefully and lovingly tended by an old man who was with the master for seventeen years. I am sure it will not be long before he is found dead on his master's bed, or on a pile of embroidered cushions.

THE DEATH OF MARGARET CASE

September 1971

Margaret was my first friend in New York. I had arrived late for a large lunch at Condé Nast's apartment and she was impressed that I had already seen the Grecos in the Hispano Museum. She showed a friendliness that few others did, and by degrees she became a very important person in my American life. She maddened me. I hated much that she said. Often her reactions showed that she did not understand what I really meant. But, my God, she was a hard-working friend. If I asked her to buy a dozen presents to take back to England, the telephone calls would continue until I was sorry I'd ever asked her. If I was in trouble she would be terribly upset. I remember when my career was threatened as a result of the Walter Winchell row, I was hard and metallic and difficult in the face of losing everything. She, the first to come round to my hotel room, sat weeping on a sofa. She realized, more than I did, what a blow had befallen me, and she was helpless to do anything for me.

Margaret was always the first person to telephone on my arrival in New York. She it was who got theatre tickets for me, reserved the table at the restaurant and was always 'at the ready' at the last minute.

Now she is dead. Perhaps in her melancholy she took an overdose, though, being a strong Roman Catholic, this does not seem likely; but whatever the reason, New York will never be the same for me. I will miss her more than I realize, and it

174

says well for her that maybe twenty other people feel the same way.

Margaret Case postscript

The sad news of her death is followed by the manner of it. It seems the unhappy soul jumped from the window of her bedroom on the fifteenth floor. One cannot imagine the misery of mind that caused her to have such terrifying last seconds.

That she suffered so much unhappiness was a shock, for Margaret seemed to have a great deal to keep her interested. I know she was upset by what was happening at *Vogue* and disturbed by the direction things were taking there; but she read a lot and she saw all the new plays. As for people, she never stopped making new friends and continued to be most loyal to her lifelong cronies. However, they obviously did not make up for the emptiness of her life; she no doubt felt that she was going round like a squirrel in a wheel, and in any case was not in a fit state to withstand any cruel blows.

The picture of her recently published is a wonderful character study of her in a benign, amused, interested mood, as she arrived as chic as-be-damned in spite of her ugly face, at some exhibition. The cameraman could not have known what emotion his picture would create in so many hearts. The sight of it went through me like a stab.

November

Nancy Mitford seems to be a bit better. She has pills which, though they make her wuzzy and silly, put her out of pain. She feels she is on the mend and may start to write her 'Souvenirs'. Should she include Mark Og's letters about the little boys he loved? Mark is dead — what harm?

But it is lovely to know that Nancy is not, as we all thought, on the way out. It is a marvel that she has survived such agony for so long; and it will be a miracle if after all she can survive a few more years.

Went to two excellent plays last week; or I should say one good play, *Butley*, and one wonderful entertainment, *The Changing Room*. David Storey, who wrote the latter, used to fly up to Manchester at the weekends to play football while studying at the Slade. He is now not only a successful novelist, but a playwright.

His subject is the behind-the-scenes at a football match, an enormous cast. I cannot think it would read well, but Lindsay Anderson has made characters of each individual, and has made it into a sort of choreographed play. The effect is stunning, for Storey knows just how to make his theatrical effects. The evening is an effective *tour de force*.

Butley is a most articulate play, in fact one I would like to read, and is made momentous by the performances by Alan Bates and Richard O'Callaghan. Bates has invented an original sense of humour. It takes a while to realize what he is up to, but by degrees one is overcome by his tongue-in-cheekness and self-mockery. He has grown his hair very shaggily long. This is obviously to compensate for the width of his neck which has now become almost inhumanly large. But what a marvellous find for the theatre he is. He came in on the new wave of John Osborne and has gone from one peak to another: a real artist, modest, determined and utterly charming.

CHANEL

Chanel is dead. One can no longer take for granted the feeling that she and her talent are always with us. She was unlike anything seen before. She was no beauty, but her appearance in the twenties and thirties was unimaginably attractive. She put all other women in the shade. Even in old age, ravaged and creased as she was, she still kept her line, and was able to put on the allure.

She used to spend most of the time complaining in her rasping, dry voice. Everyone except her was at fault. But you were doing her a service by remaining in her presence, for even her most loyal friends had been forced to leave her. You tried to leave, too, for your next appointment, but she had perfected the technique of delaying you. Her flow of talk could not be interrupted. You rose from your seat and made backwards for the door. She followed. Her face ever closer to yours. Then you were out on the landing and down a few stairs. The rough voice still went on. Then you blew a kiss. She knew now that loneliness again faced her. She smiled a goodbye. The mouth stretched in a grimace, but from a distance it worked the old magic.

I found myself outside the shop a few weeks ago. I had not seen her since the musical *Coco* and thought I'd pay her a call. She looked older than ever. No gipsy had ever looked so old. The hair was like black wool; eye-black smudged; no make-up would remain on the dark skin. Her hands appeared enormous at the ends of long, stringy arms. The chest was almost concave. She never ate anything; one felt that it was only her spirit that kept her going. Her servants and the others who work for her were cowed. But she knew that she would always have the whip hand.

I always wanted to get to know Coco, but she was very forbidding. She never had any feelings of friendship for me, so I am not disloyal when I write of her venom, her lack of generosity and her disloyalty.

For fifty years she went on proving that her taste was impeccable. She had a strong, daring, sure approach that made others fade into insignificance; never anything extraneous and fussy; she believed in utter simplicity. She was a female Brummell. Just as the Beau got rid of frills and furbelows overnight, so too Chanel demonstrated that nothing was more chic than fine linen, navy-blue serge and lots of soap. She had an eye to quality and proportion that was unbeatable. She had daring, freshness, authenticity, conviction. She was exceptional and she knew it. She was unfeminine in character, but totally feminine in her ability to entice, and she had great sex appeal. Chanel had qualities and talents that are very rare. She was a genius, and all her faults must be forgiven for that one reason.

London: Saturday, December 18th

It is very seldom that I am in London at the weekends, but I wanted to go to the memorial service for Gladys Cooper on Saturday.

The service was beautifully arranged. Stanley Holloway read from the *Pilgrim's Progress*; A Shakespeare sonnet on 'Love' was read by Celia Johnson; a serenade from *Hassan* played; Robert Morley's comic and evocative address gave great relief to the congregation and prevented the atmosphere becoming morbid. A prayer, a blessing, then two minutes of silence in which we were all to remember, in our own way, our friend Gladys.

For myself, I remember Gladys since, as a faltering schoolboy, I went up to her when she was having lunch at the Carlton Restaurant with Gertie Millar. I remember the sweetness with which she acceded to my stammering request, and said I must of course also ask for the signature of her friend. Her complexion was of a white and pink marshmallow perfection, her hair fair silky fluff and eyes the bluest.

Gladys — I could now write a book about her. She was one of the recurring enthusiasms in my life. She has meant a great deal to me. I was full of admiration for the way she could be *utterly* herself on all occasions. Few people have had such strength of character. Gladys had her share of disappointments and tragedies, but she accepted everything with a wide-eyed courage.

As Sybil Thorndike was about to be driven away from the church, I told her how beautiful she had become, more so now than at any time in her life. 'Don't be such a fool! Don't be so silly!' she said, but was pleased. Then she said, 'I hope my service will be as gay as this one. It won't be long now; you know I'm nearly ninety!' and waving and leaning back and cackling, away she went.

Kitty Miller during a dragging conversation said: 'I knew Proust.' Suddenly everyone was on the edge of their seats. 'Tell us what was he like?' Kitty answered: 'Ghastly, darling!'

Reddish: December

A quiet weekend with David and Caroline Somerset. I met a lot of old friends and when I left I felt refreshed and pleased at having had such a 'different' time.

The return journey to Broadchalke was delightful. Motored to Bath, and caught the train to Salisbury and suddenly realized how pleasant a country train journey can be. One sees so comparatively little driving a motor-car.

This is one of my favourite parts of England. Bath is always a surprise treat and today, although mid-winter and grey weather, it looked as beautiful as ever in the silver mist, and the countryside around Bradford-on-Avon was feathery and sylvan.

The stone cottages among the undulating hills are beautifully harmonious in the landscape. Even at this bleak time of the year the willows were lovely and the cottage kitchen-gardens had patches of brilliant green among the grey; a real delight to wind along in the slow-moving train with the river near at hand.

I was in a good holiday mood, coming back to my home for a long spell. Smallpeice greeted me with the news that the Wilton Hunt had met at Broadchalke. They were in the village street when suddenly they saw a fox rushing towards them from our new water garden. The fox leapt the wall, ran through the wrought-iron gate into the garden and straight over the lawn to the paddock with the hounds in full pursuit. No damage was done but Claire Pembroke was acutely embarrassed; we all thought it very funny; hearty laughter on all sides.

January 1972

'Sir' is a romantic title. It sounds so unlike me, so much less personal than 'Mr Beaton'. 'Sir' on envelopes seems to take away some individuality, but I felt proud, and sorry that my mother was not alive to share my pleasure.

A VISIT TO EGYPT

Cairo: March

Mercifully one is apt to remember only the high-spots of one's travels; the things of great beauty not seen before. But few of us, when setting off for the far corners, realize what hours, even days, are to be spent standing at some airline reception desk and, even if successful in getting tickets, what further long delays in airport lounges are to be endured.

But never in my experience, or in Raymond Mortimer's, has there been such gruelling, nerve-wracking incompetence at points of arrival and departure as in present-day Egypt. The tourist invasion has led to complete chaos. Scheduled trips are carefully arranged, but, just to give one example, the likelihood is that one hundred people may arrive at midnight from London only to be told that half their number will be without rooms as the government has commandeered them.

Appalling to wake up to see the ugliness of Cairo today. Skyscrapers everywhere and the minareted silhouettes gone for ever; modern blocks of the cheapest cement cheek by jowl with the mosques; the whole town a beastly modern, anonymous mess. Such desecrations cannot be imagined.

Wednesday, March 8th

To the Aswan Lake to see the Temple of Philae. This was a wonderful, romantic expedition. We sailed along a dark passage, past a large, carved woman's head, into the sunlight to see the Ptolemaic carvings on the walls each side of the entrance to the inner sanctum. Although these figures have been defaced by Copts or Moslems, they are still of an extraordinary beauty. It was exciting to see them as they were planned to be seen perhaps five thousand years ago. But the effect was made more strange by the water coming up to the thigh level on a row of rotund women, all that remained visible of a colonnade. Here was an Egyptian Venice, full of unaccustomed effects; water where there should have been sand. The effect of their reflections in the water was bizarre and theatrical.

The Cataract Hotel

A serene night's sleep with soothing, entertaining dreams; a sense of well-being. Headaches a thing of the past. Early call. As expected, a rush to get off the boat to see the Temple of Kom Ombo. It was built for two different gods at the same time on a plan that divided the building in equal sections.

In the early morning sunlight the carved walls were at their best. The details and fantasy were quite varied: someone being fed, a lion eating a crocodile, a boat full of papyrus with birds among royal cartouches; huge slender feet next to a frieze of animal-headed personages; each wall decorated being a tribute to Ptolemy, father of *our* Cleopatra, who built the imposing colonnades, halls and perfume shops; all of *crème caramel* stone.

Even if one is not particularly partial to the Egyptian style, this temple is in its own way utterly successful, not only for the beauty of the drawing, the exquisite purity and quality of draughtsmanship, but in the general planning, so that the sun shines on columns and walls just as in the manner intended and gives the necessary colour to the bas reliefs.

Luxor

Well here I am, fly whisk on table, wearing shorts and a large, straw hat. I am looking around at the enormous pineapples of bougainvillaea that cascade from the top of two vast palms. Formal flowerbeds are full of hibiscus, salvia, cactus, gerbera, ferns, and hollyhocks. The trees are gargantuan; to me they are nameless but beautiful and are a dark haven to thousands of doves and all sorts of singing and twittering birds.

But there are even disappointments here. I had imagined the hotel as being white with lots of Arabic decoration delicately cut out in wood. Instead it is heavy and solid and deep cedar-coloured and has a new swimming pool to which all the tourists migrate. However, it is an oasis from the squalor of the town, the shopping lanes, and the touts.

The climate is ideal. Yet I am not at all content. It is awful to see a country that is going to the dogs, that is living in and on the past. Tours by *caleche*, bus, and boat have shown us the best of this country. But having spent most of the morning battling with hall porters and tour guides, and being bitten by flies while I wait in dreary offices and undergo infinite humiliations, I have become disgruntled. Perhaps I hate too much.

Peter, our chief guide, proved to be a little, elderly Egyptian Jean Cocteau. He was remarkably thin with the skin of his face stretched tightly over beautiful bones. His amused expression conveyed, with raised eyebrows and pursed thin lips, resignation and sorrow. He used his hands to great effect; they became beautiful in movement as he demonstrated a point or wielded his cane. He was a dandy. He wore a tarboosh and, over a white jellabah, a natty brown jacket of smart European cut. He showed a great deal of white cuff.

Peter spoke in quite perfect, even rather precious, English. He said that some of the more brash American tourists had difficulty in understanding him. For a man who is a serious scholar it must be a burden to have to spend so much of his time escorting people with little knowledge of Egypt and her history.

We walked in a leisurely manner to the Temple of Luxor. In the morning light it appeared more magnificent than at dusk when it had looked dusty and unimpressive. Peter pointed out with his walking-stick various felicities, the mixture of style, obelisks, minarets, and Roman arch all together within the same outer walls.

Upper Egypt

It was unusually exciting to drive through high cliffs knowing that we were about to see the tombs where the Pharaohs are buried, with all the golden treasures they considered they should have, together with furniture, jewels, foods and comforts for their after-life.

They had taken such care that their earthly remains should not be discovered or their presents to the gods plundered, that they employed mostly blind workers to dig their graves. But after 3,000 years these had been unearthed. Howard Carter and Lord Carnarvon made the great discovery of Tutankhamun's tomb. Imagine the excitement when they looked through a wall at jewels hidden for so long. They saw, gleaming in the half darkness, the life-size figure of a jackal, a symbol of death, gold caskets, jewelled mummies, and golden beds carved with sacred animals.

We drove high into the dust-coloured mountain and then were conducted to the tomb of Rameses IX, perhaps one of the biggest and certainly the most beautiful that we saw. Fascinating details of contemporary life were painted on the walls, illustrations depicting the sun, the Pharaoh symbol, on its journey to the underworld and its final resurrection. In one large chamber the goddess Night, my favourite, with arms and body like a snake, decorated the ceiling of dark blue and gold.

Cairo: Tea with Madame Fouad

An evening was spent visiting Madame Fouad, a Turkish hostess who was a great figure during the war and entertained lavishly in a huge house. She had a nilometer at the bottom of her garden with which the depth of the river could be measured. Now much of her influence has gone but she has battled with the regime successfully enough to have most of her confiscated possessions returned. But they did not give her back the furniture which had been placed traditionally in her tomb in the City of the Dead in preparation for her demise.

Her house, rather large for one old girl, is now a ghastly mixture of good and bad, dotted with relics of the past; beautiful Persian needlework caskets, china, and medieval brass. All was in need of a good dusting. The glass of the chandeliers was caked with dirt. It was a sad sight. So was she, an anachronism, but through guts and courage she has succeeded in living the life she wants.

STAYING WITH MICKY RENSHAW IN CYPRUS

March 17th

The joy of finding myself in this highly civilized house was beyond anything. The landscape of high ranges of jagged and wooded mountains, groves of carab and olive, and tall, pale, lush green grasses was beautiful. I was delighted at the prospect of remaining in the same bedroom for an indeterminate stay.

The sight from my windows in the early morning when the shutters were drawn made me gasp; every sort of blue, green, and yellow on the hills dotted with gorse, broom, and mustard, all in bloom. In few places could I have relaxed and recuperated in such comfort. Breakfast of crisp, fresh bread was an extreme pleasure. My cold, caught in Egypt, became bronchitis and I was as weak as an invalid, but I enjoyed listening to the music of Mahler on the record-player while Micky went about his chores.

The expedition into Kyrenia with Micky was delightful, the market full of the most appetizing-looking fruits, all oversized; lemons like gourds, oranges, and tangerines; vegetables exotic; vast artichokes, the first asparagus, pale ivory balls of cabbage.

I loved seeing the wild flowers and other people's gardens. We went on expeditions to Salamis, Morphou, Vouni; wandered in the remains of a rich Persian's palace and through the Laurence Durrell countryside of Bellapaix and the marvellous ruins of a Romanesque monastery. We took my godson, Caspar Fleming, to excavate at Neolithic sites.

WEST GERMANY

May 19th

Went to Essen — clean, calm, quiet, tree-lined avenues, good shops — to see the reconstructed cathedral. Disappointing on the whole; this was possibly because most of its treasures had been lent to the medieval exhibition we saw at Cologne.

But the Museum Folkwang with modern pictures shown in juxtaposition with ancient Egyptian objects was full of delight, and I'm sorry my eagle eyes missed many things picked out by Liliane Rothschild, such as a painting by Manet of soldiers being killed. The Renoir of a huge and ugly woman in white muslin made one realize what real painting is like; a yellow water-lily scene by Monet, very strange and rare.

The collection is a combination of State and Krupp; a son of the family welcomed us, and then took us on with his

American wife, to see the family mansion, Villa Hügel — an ugly house.

An hour's bus ride took us to Wasserburg to see Vischering, a very romantic castle, dating from 1550, surrounded by water; heraldic shutters, old rose brick and empty inside.

May 20th

Quite a long ride to Soest, a delightful little medieval town; many houses were covered with black and white beams, had fans over the doors and harlequin shutters; some of the old roofs had been cleverly restored after war damage. The verdigris on the walls of the cathedral, the Gothic church of Notre Dame des Champs, and other stone buildings created a theatrical 'powdered' effect. Then a delightful meander through the market, buying a bunch of freesias for Nancy Lancaster; and lunch in an old-fashioned Wilder Mann restaurant.

Sitting alone in the bus and not talking is my greatest pleasure and this afternoon I was in an ecstasy as we drove through hilly country planted with straight and healthy trees, pale youthful green contrasting with the dark of the pines. The Germans are good foresters, and on this late-spring afternoon the greenness and the leaves of last autumn making a smooth russet carpet was very beautiful.

I saw a boy of not more than six, clean and pink-and-white skinned, in charge of a huge herd of beige and white cows. He smiled and waved gaily at us until, with anxiety, he saw one of his beasts going astray. His sense of responsibility was at once apparent. You could see clearly that he had been brought up to know how important it was to take care of the means of his family's livelihood.

We visited an eighteenth-century jesuit baroque church at Büren with decoration by Cuvilliés; beautifully proportioned windows of clear glass and the sun slanting through made a striking, dramatic effect.

A long drive to Château d'Arolsen, an imitation Versailles. The exterior with the twin porters' lodges and caved-in tiled roofs was interesting. The Château was built by a prince but it seems the money ran out before it was finished. We laughed a great deal at some of the Edwardian and Victorian furniture, portraits, and bedroom utensils. The 'oriental' room was very amusing, the huge ballroom unbelievably ugly. The Tischbein portraits and some good tapestries saved the day. We walked in the azalea gardens and on terraces and thought of Conder's fans.

A short ride through more beautiful, sharp green trees to Kassel. The vast schloss of Wilhelmshöhe unimaginably grand in scale. We strolled in the very large gardens, and saw cascades falling from the mountain top on which there is a gigantic figure of Hercules. I loved watching the light fade in this quiet, still, false romanticism; not one frond of a branch moved.

Sunday

Started off in spring sunshine with lowering clouds for the super romantic château of Lowenburg. The dungeon was bombed by us in the last war thus adding to the artificial 'ruin' effect. Some rooms were very small and pretty and contained good glass, pictures, and objects; a circular room, with red velvet on the walls, looking over a vast panorama. The beech hedges in the garden were an inspiration to Nancy Lancaster, who was determined to copy them in her own garden.

In pouring torrents to the Musée de Hesse, a wonderful collection of paintings, porcelain, silver-gilt, and nineteen

Rembrandts, including one of an old man in black velvet painted when the artist was thirty.

Hanover: May 23rd

The bus driver is gentle, clever, and imaginative. The sun was very hot today, and while we waited to see the Le Notre-esque gardens of Herrenhausen, designed at the end of the eighteenth century, the guide, as usual, went on too long, so the driver gently moved forward to the shade of some avenues. Later in the day he manoeuvred the bus through arches with only an inch to spare each side so that the occupants all applauded.

The gardens were well worth waiting for, quite wonderful parterres laid out with black and white pansies, a triumph of artifice, nature completely subjugated to man's whims; statues, hedges, gravel in baroque shapes. We were then received by the Prince and Princess of Hanover who were standing in the garden of a very pretty little house which they have now turned into a museum. My friend Felix Harbord had redecorated it and had helped to save some of the furniture which now adorns these beautifully proportioned rooms. The Princess has an eye for colour and the enfilade was extremely effective with red, yellow, green, and blue rooms full of gilt-framed pictures. The dining-room had enormous paintings of the family and their entourage, the keeper of the falcons and owls, and other servants, framed in white on green backgrounds; very successful.

Arrival at the extraordinary 'new' medieval castle of Marienburg, built in the English nineteenth-century style. Here again we were escorted by the Hanovers who showed us their magnificent collection of Georgian silver, tables, chairs, mirrors, and cupboards full of wine containers, canisters, beakers, and bowls. We peered into every bedroom and nook and looked at every photograph. We then went to the farmhouse where the Hanovers now live in severe simplicity. Decorated with charm and no pretension, the house is part of a huge farm complex made up of blue and white painted buildings and a duck pond.

Hamburg

In the wind and the rain we drove through flat country to reborn Hamburg. Our guide feels no self-pity for the bombing of his country, but told us that over ninety per cent of Hamburg had been destroyed in 'saturation bombing', that one night the fiery holocaust sent the inhabitants fleeing to the river, but the huge fire bombs set the water alight and thousands were burnt in the sulphurous flames.

The Germans are an extraordinary race; sentimental, musical, law abiding, but cruel beyond imagination. They have a determination to survive which manifests itself in no small measure in the Hamburg of today, an entirely new industrial town of great richness. Its inhabitants thrive and do business with people from all over the world.

Lanfranco Rasponi and I went to the new huge opera house to hear *Don Carlos*, and later we 'went on the town' and walked down the Broadway area where all the sex shows and bordellos are situated along and off the Reeperbahn.

Lubeck: May 27th

It was what I saw in the Museum of St Anne at Lubeck that made me feel that all this effort of travel had been worthwhile. It was a miraculous altar-piece by Hans Memling; a triptych of the Passion of Christ. The picture was strange and wonderful, the Mother Mary so sorrowful, the Christ so pitiful, the green ground littered with odd-shaped bones, the tufts of growth, flowers, and herbs, the sanctity of expression on the faces of the men witnesses to the scenes. All were painted with tenderness, delicacy, and a consistency of love. I felt I had really been enriched. My heart went out to Memling, and to Lubeck and its museum.

Paris: May 28th

I woke early to hear Lilia Ralli's familiar chirp announcing the death of the Duke of Windsor. I felt callously indifferent, no pang of nostalgia. Certainly he had been a great figure in my adolescence, full of charm and dash, glamorous, and a good Prince of Wales. Then the sensational abdication and marriage. As a photographer, I came into that scene in a big way, but throughout the years the Duke had never shown any affection for or interest in me. In fact, perhaps rather presumptuously, I felt he disliked me. It was only at the last meeting when I went to have a drink with 'Darby and Joan', and all his men friends were dead, that he thawed towards me, and talked about the 'old times'. He was always cold in his friendships, and could cut them off overnight. He was inclined to be silly. When James Pope-Hennessy told him he was writing a book about Trollope, he roared with laughter and turned to Wallis saying: "E's writing a book about a trollop!'

I am sorry for the Duchess. She will be sad. Another milestone passed.

Windsor

The Duke's funeral was noble and dignified. The military knights in their scarlet uniforms, medals clinking, marched with a loud stamp-shuffle. The slowness and the muffled metal sound was impressive, and the fact that these knights were all aged, with clear pink skins, made it that much more remarkable.

The coffin, borne by eight sturdy Welsh Guardsmen, arms linked and heads bowed, was draped with the Duke's personal standard, and covered with a huge trembling mass of Madonna lilies. Members of the Royal Family followed; the King of Norway, extra tall; the Duke of Edinburgh, grey and drawn and yet emitting strength; the delightful, charming young Prince of Wales; the young Kents and Gloucesters; and Lord Mountbatten.

The service was short and poignant. An anthem. Prayers. Another hymn, then a dramatic moment when Garter King of Arms read out the Styles and Titles of the late Duke: Knight of the Garter, Knight of the Thistle, King Edward VIII of England, Ruler of India ... and the ribbons and badges of the orders were carried on cushions. One was reminded of Shakespeare's kings and princes.

Majorca: August

Am really sorry for myself. So far I've enjoyed more than average good health, but lately a blight has been put on my existence by my not being able to read or write without being punished with a nervous head pain that stretches over my left eye, over the head and down the nape of my neck. It puts such a damper on my activities. I live by my eyes. It is being particularly annoying during the holiday when there is little to do but read.

Dr Gottfried does not seem optimistic. He says that the headache is caused by the arteries to the brain getting tight, due to brain fag and overstrain. I have been many times to excellent oculists and they say there is nothing wrong with my eyes, that eye strain does not exist. However, I do know that if I have used my eyes more than average, the pain strikes. It is very hard to know what to do, especially when I had hoped my old age would be spent reading and writing if not painting.

Visited the Cuevas del Aria: huge, cavernous grottoes, millions of years old with stalactites and stalagmites that have taken all these aeons of time to form; one's mind boggles.

It was cool, damp and dark, but the stalactites and stalagmites were lit theatrically with coloured lights.

With a jolly guide to show sightseers around, he turned the lights off for a moment and created havoc. The terror of finding oneself lost here would be enough to cause one's heart to stop. Then the lights were turned on full to red and a hidden orchestra blared out Wagner.

I thought immediately of the theatre, for this is the sort of stage effect that we no longer see there: magical and mysterious. I long to see a Shakespearean production given an elaborate, imaginative setting. This would be an inspiration for *The Tempest*. I would be thrilled to design such a production with sculpted torrents and flags and Renaissance candlesticks all made of some new fibre fabric. It could be transparent and give infinite varieties of light against this elaborate background. The costumes would be very simple, in basic colours, mostly white, grey, blue, green. Only the masque characters would be in gold and silver.

NOËL AT 'LES AVANTS'

Montreux: September 1972

I had heard about Noël's Swiss retreat. 'It's very typical of him, lots of signed photographs, a house that might have been brought from Eastbourne.' It is true the house suits Noël perfectly. It has no real character, is ugly, is decorated in the typical theatre-folk style, but it is warm and comfortable and it works.

I found Noël in a scarlet jacket hunched and crumpled in a chair, looking very old and resigned and fatter. He seemed a bit surprised to see me although, no doubt, as he later said, he had been looking forward to my visit. A glass of brandy and ginger-ale was within reach and the cigarettes at hand. Noël is only a bit more than seventy. He suffers from a bad leg; the circulation cannot be relied upon and if he walks he can be in great pain. As a result, he doesn't walk, and spends most of his time in bed. This is not good for anyone. But Noël has aged into a very nice and kind old man. He is really a darling, so trim and neat, his memory unfailing. His intelligence was as quick as ever and within a few moments we were enjoying each others' jokes and laughing a lot.

You know that when Noël gives an evaluation of someone else's talent or personality, he will be absolutely 'on the ball' and never prejudiced. There are certain types that he despises. He has no time for amateurs, or people that tell lies or are phoneys. But he is incredibly generous in his appreciation of most people, particularly those who have succeeded in the theatre.

Naturally we reminisced about the first times we met; how he gave me a deserved 'going over' during a return journey from America, and more recently about the production of *Quadrille*. He complimented me on my professionalism and said I was a most direct and workmanlike designer.

Later in the evening it was wonderful to hear him singing in a quiet but musical voice the songs that had meant so much to him since he was a boy. Noël still remembers all the lyrics;

Vesta Tilley songs, Albert Chevalier songs from a terrible Jack Hulbert musical called *The Light Blues* in which Noël had learnt to tap dance, and snatches of songs from long-forgotten musicals.

I asked Noël to tell me about the stars he had seen from the pit when taken to the theatre by his mother on birthday treats. 'Lily Elsie, the way she moved, very slowly, but with incredible grace; those long arms and never a coy gesture. She was such fun too — a darling! And her voice true.' Of Gertie Millar: 'She could dance like a wisp, with those long legs, and she was a star and like all stars she had vitality. No one without vitality can have any glamour.' He talked lovingly of Gertie Lawrence, as someone with whom he could never quarrel for she was such a perfectionist. He had great praise for Maisie Gay, whom he considered more a brilliant dramatic actress than a comedienne. She played each part as if it were written by Chekhov.

It was time to go to bed. In the lift, recently built for Noël's comfort, he plopped himself down on the stool and said, 'It's awful. I'm so old!'

Visit to Vaynol: October 1972

Vaynol used to be the centre of much frivolity and inspired gaiety; charades, improvisations, elaborate dressing-up, practical jokes, youthful gaiety of all sorts. Now two wings of about thirty rooms have been pulled down. It has become more and more difficult for Michael[11] to maintain the place as in the old days.

Michael has a very busy life attending to his various responsibilities, so, because he was at a meeting, we were met at the station by the old chauffeur; an old butler came out of

---

[11] Sir Michael Duff.

the front door as we drove up, made a little speech regretting Michael's absence, and then said that the first time he had seen me was in 1936! Patrick Procktor on hearing this was staggered, as it was the year of his birth, and I could not believe that forty years had passed since I first came to this house. So the visit took on the colour of a journey into the past.

Soon Michael appeared and cheered us with the readiness of his interest, his curiosity, his humour. For someone who started as a backward child, he has come a long way and has made a very interesting life for himself. He and I have shared so much of the past together that we necessarily veered towards subjects that we had both enjoyed.

In the house there were many bibelots and pieces of furniture that had belonged to Michael's mother, Juliet. Juliet's scrapbooks were brought out and I was staggered that the well-remembered events here recorded had taken place so long ago. It seemed to me as if they had happened but yesterday. It was with a haunted fascination that we looked at those old milestones. People who had to us seemed so old and decrepit then, now appeared to look young, and even beautiful.

Michael gave me a feeling of strength. He has survived well, so why shouldn't I? He had no regrets, so why should I feel sad. Maybe it had all been frivolous, but it had been a creative frivolity, and it must have taught one something about certain aspects of life. Anyhow it was no use sighing.

BABA'S ILLNESS

November

New York — St Regis; breakfast just begun when telephone rings unexpectedly early. It is my brother-in-law, Hugh, from

England with a note of anxiety in his voice. Obviously he was very emotionally het-up: 'It's about Baba. You know they examined her and thought it gall trouble.' 'Yes, yes.' 'Well she's had an operation, but they find she has cancer of the pancreas, and they can't do anything about it. She may last another two weeks, but they're going to keep her under sedation. They're going to tell her. We all think she'd prefer it to us all telling her a lot of lies.'

How terrible! How terrible! I now know what we had all feared and it is worse than we could have imagined. Up until now my sister Baba has never been ill for a day. She has always been strong; but she has been sad, her life never really a happy one. Her husband was killed in the war and much of the time since she has spent being brave and making excuses for her loneliness. Her lover, after twenty-five years, went off without a word. Baba became ill.

A piece of my childhood is about to disappear.

Hawarden Castle: March 1973

As the doctor prophesied, Baba's condition has slowly deteriorated. She has come up to be with her beloved daughter, Rosamund, for the last time. She is desperately weak but she has not given in, and it makes her angry that she is not strong enough to come down to lunch, write her name, or light a cigarette.

She looks incredibly beautiful; so thin as to be hardly recognizable; the bone formation of her face is marvellous, high cheekbones, noble nose and brow, and her forehead is without wrinkles.

I am somewhat comforted to see that death need not be as terrifying as one feared. The sedatives make the withering away less tragic; her fading out will be like that of a plant which suddenly becomes sick.

Sunday, March 11th
I steeled myself. The first thing that struck me on entering her room, and I saw her lying asleep with her face turned towards the window, was that her hair had fallen on to her forehead. This somehow added the final touch of poignancy to the picture. It affected me deeply.

I stared at Baba. She lay, a small steel grey piece of sculpture, and I left the room in a state of complete breakdown.

Almost a week later
Rosamund telephoned early in the morning. Baba had died at 4 am. Goodbye Baba, who was always so independent, so lithe and graceful; always with a pet dog, so athletic and country loving.

Goodbye my most beautiful first, home-made model. Goodbye to so much of my own life. Goodbye to Baba.

New York: March
A painless radio interview; talked mostly about Picasso; then a marvellously easy lunch with Lincoln Kirstein who is always full of spicy good news. He took me to the Lincoln Library of the Performing Arts and showed me all the De Meyer photographs of Nijinsky. They were the first poetical ballet pictures.

Lincoln, with great modesty, for he had found and donated most of them, showed me the exhibition of the library's latest acquisitions; Diaghilev's payroll lists and expenses; a drawing by Fragonard; eighteenth-century coloured engravings by Berain; masks, gloves, a Stravinsky telegram, and a marvellous drawing of an Etruscan corseted figure in the notebook that Bakst took on his first visit to Greece.

Reddish: June 16th

The summer weather is so unbelievably beautiful that I only wish my sense of delight and enjoyment was stronger. Perhaps, after a day or two's rest, I will regain my zest. Already I feel less tired, and have been out in the early morning sun walking barefoot on the dew-covered lawns. The birds are having a fine time (the pigeons very destructive!) and the doves seem to have made a haunt of this place. We saw a kingfisher down in the water-garden and there are chaffinches and yellow hammers. The garden is at its peak. Just *before* its best, Clarissa[12] came and had tea under an awning on the terrace, and thought she liked the garden best now when you could see the shapes before all the colour. The terrace is a mass of roses, and I only trust the summer will continue till next weekend when the garden is open!'

MARLENE DIETRICH

I watched on television Marlene Dietrich's successful performance staged at Drury Lane. The quality of the photography was extraordinarily exact, and I felt I saw more and heard more than if I had been a part of the wildly enthusiastic audience. As for Marlene, aged seventy (actresses are always said to be older than they are), she was quite a remarkable piece of artifice. Somehow she has evolved an agelessness. Even for a hardened expert like myself, it was impossible to find the chink in her armour. All the danger spots were disguised. Her dress, her figure, her limbs, all gave

---

[12] Countess of Avon.

the illusion of youth. The high cheekbones remain intact, the forehead good, the deep-set eyelids useful attributes, and she does the rest.

Not much of a never-musical voice is left, but her showmanship persists. Marlene has become a sort of mechanical doll. The doll can show surprise, it can walk, it can swish into place the train of its white fur coat. The audience applauds each movement, each gesture. The doll smiles incredulously. Can it really be for me that you applaud? Again a very simple gesture, maybe the hands flap, and again the applause, not just from old people who remembered her tawdry films, but the young, too, who find her sexy. She is louche and not averse to giving a slight wink.

Marlene has created another career for herself and is certainly a great star, not without talent, and with a genius for believing in her self-fabricated beauty.

Her success is out of all proportion and yet it is entirely due to her perseverance that she is not just an old discarded film star. She magnetizes her audience and mesmerises them (and herself) into believing in her.

I sat enraptured and not a bit critical as I had imagined I might be. The old trooper never changes her tricks because she knows they work, and because she invented them.

Villa Albrizzi, Este: August 23rd, 1973
Peering into the same bowl in the art nouveau bathroom, and seeing the old stain of rust on the rim of the loo, made me realize that nothing whatsoever has changed since I was last here three years ago. Yet much had happened to me during that time.

But what had I done with the time, except misuse it by being, as Oscar Wilde said of the Americans, 'In too great a hurry to catch trains'? I had done a hell of a lot of work, and some of it well paid, but in no other way was it of much avail.

I had been to foreign parts and seen a *d'egringolade* take place in the United States. In the country, several pleasant additions had been made to house and garden. But horrid things also had occurred. Due to what specialists say does not exist, yet I am convinced does, eyestrain continues to give me headaches.

Perhaps the greatest change has taken place within myself as I steer towards my seventieth birthday. Most noticeable, apart from thinning hair, a paunch, paleness of eye, is the attitude of the young towards me. 'Will you be tired if we do that? Let me fetch it. I'll drive.' So far I have not yet noticed a deterioration in my drawing or in my powers to write; certainly my reading has dwindled. But although I do not embark on a holiday with the same eagerness that I used to and do know that during these weeks I am not likely to fall in love, or make new friends, I am grateful that, either from my father or my mother, I have inherited a strong body and a system that withstands many trials. When I look at certain contemporaries, those that have survived, I am appalled to see how they have become prematurely old.

A day's trip to Mantua, in the great heat, knocked me out to such an extent that for several days I remained at the villa idling, very *familial* and remote from the outer world. It was like a bolt from the blue when George Weidenfeld arrived hot from his latest romance in Venice, via Israel and the South of France, with all the international news and gossip. It seems the pound has gone lower than before, that England is considered as a faded, leisurely old-fashioned country as Italy was once by Henry James; that the Austrians and Germans have the strongest currency; that Germany and France are loathing one another.

George told us that Kissinger was now Secretary of State, that Nixon gave a clever press interview in which he said the amount of bugging he did was nothing to that done by his predecessors, and that Nixon's unpopularity had turned, and that he would survive to be a popular president.

George's vitality and curiosity are unquenchable. He is good value, shrewd, and fair. He makes me feel rut-ridden and sluggish. Little wonder that he has swept all before him and seems to have the best of so many worlds.

Staying with Mrs Joseph Lambert: September 1973

The others went off to Venice to watch the Regatta, and I had the day to myself. It was like a purge.

I walked around the garden, watched the swans and looked for a vantage point for sketching. I sat on a seat. The day was blissful, no wind stirred, not too hot a sun. I gave up the idea of sketching and for the first time in a long while remained just sitting. For a long time I was occupied with my thoughts and a few ideas came into my overcrowded, blocked-up brain. I thought a bit about my future and my work and what best to do. I thought about the work in hand, and one or two little improvements came filtering through. I wished I had more time for sitting and meditating at Broadchalke.

Lunch served in an elaborate manner in which the Italians excel; gazpacho, omelette, ice-cream, and cheese. I watched the ripples on the nearby pool. There was, as I have said, very little breeze, and everything seemed still. Yet in the shade of the trees tongues of light ran down the plane tree trunks, and occasionally an unseen gust caused some low-hanging branches of acacia to be dipped in the water, then, dripping, they were released, and the water was motionless again. A leaf fell on to its surface and the reflections were still until a fish poked up at a fly, and caused circles to flow outwards in a symmetrical design. This made the reflections move in a ballet-like rhythm; a hard, sharp, straight twig became a reflected corkscrew, then a rhythmic whip, then, slowly, it regained its sharp monogynous image.

It was fascinating to watch the activity in this silent, motionless spot. As I got up to walk away, a lot of small, unseen frogs leapt from the bordering grass to disappear in the shallow water.

CYRIL CONNOLLY'S SEVENTIETH BIRTHDAY

London: September 11th

Cyril was only told the *venue* at the last minute as the car turned into Regent's Park and went on to the Zoo. Because of the heatwave, his friends gathered outdoors at the members' club drinking champagne. John Betjeman, with trousers too short, walking like a toddler on the sands; he only lacked a bucket and spade. Alastair Forbes, Anthony Powell, Hamish Hamilton, eight people from *The Sunday Times* and Raymond Mortimer, in old age looking beautiful with long wavy silver hair. To comfort those of us who are reaching the age of seventy, Raymond said that he had been happier during the last five years (he is seventy-five) than at any other time of his life. He certainly looks contented, serene, unworried.

Philippe de Rothschild, Anne Fleming, Antony Hobson and Tania were there, and, of course, Deirdre. Deirdre told me that Cyril reads in bed almost all day. He hardly ever goes out and at Eastbourne they see no one. Cyril's life is entirely centred round his books, but it seems an interesting, satisfying life.

Cyril looked calm, pretty as a celluloid cupid in a bath, with no apparent nervousness, and although he says he has never made a speech, did in fact deliver himself of a spontaneous one. It was a typical piece of Cyril embroidery about his having an unhappy childhood (only son) with ill-assorted parents, how as a schoolboy he went to St Cyprian's, 'where a younger boy, Beaton, he was only called Beaton, taught me about painting and we ate gooseberries together — when the black ones were finished, we ate the green ones. When the unhappy only son of ill-assorted parents went on to another school, here he attained puberty and he admired the shell-like ear of a boy with black hair, Noel Blakiston and he's sitting over there, and then I won a scholarship for Eton and I became friends with Kenneth Clark, sitting over there. Then I worked in J. C. Squire's office and was helped by J. B. Betjeman — and he's sitting over there; and Tony Powell helped me and he's sitting over there.' We thought he might be going through the whole thirty-odd guests and making it a 'This Is Your Life', but it was perfectly timed and not a sentence too long. It was funny, pithy, satirical, well dramatized — Cyril at his best; a lovely celebration.

VISIT TO DADIE RYLANDS AT KING'S

December 1973

I had seen Dadie two weeks ago at Raymond Mortimer's at Crichel and was struck by his healthiness, his freshness, vigour, and purity.

I thought him wonderfully rare and uncontaminated by the rush and squalor of contemporary life. Only occasionally does he take wing from his life of books and study, but whenever he does make friendly forays, he always shows a childlike enjoyment.

Extraordinary as it seems, Dadie is now over seventy. He still appears to me, even if a bit thinner on top, to be the young bullocky blond that he was at King's when I was unhappily at St John's.

Dadie was, with his pale-blue eyes, blue tie, pink-and-white complexion, and canary quiff of hair, a spectacular figure. A great friend of all the Bloomsbury group, the names of Lytton, Duncan, Vanessa, and Clive were seldom off his lips. He was loved and passionate; his reputation was most enviable. He played the Duchess of Malfi, a role that I could have performed if only I had not been so tiresome and difficult, and it was the best Duchess of Malfi I have seen, out of at least a dozen. Dadie was dignified like a unicorn, neither male nor female.

Now Dadie, in boyish open neck, welcomed Jakie Astor and me in his kitchen. I have seldom seen anything so ordered in the clutter of his rooms, a magpie's hoard of silver, china, and twenty-ish paintings. Mercifully everything was extremely well dusted and polished. Nevertheless, the effect was peculiar, a mixture of a Victorian old lady's taste and donnish severity; mahogany bookcases, china cabinets, and a hangover of Bloomsbury décor. Carrington had painted typical and pretty panels on the doors and cupboards, and his smaller sitting-room was liberally sprinkled with 'dated' nudes against a noughts-and-crosses background.

Dadie made the tea, produced hot buttered buns and macaroons. He asked about Jakie's 'arable land', gave information about what all the Cambridge celebrities were doing and how they had achieved eminence in other fields. He was quick and trenchant and showed a wide range of interest; his little beady eyes popping and his lips pressed in a pout as he listened. One felt that time had in no way impaired the sharpness of his brain. He talked about Thomas Hardy, quite a close family connection there; about Siegfried Sassoon, and Stephen Tennant, Victor Rothschild, and Raymond Mortimer, all of whom he described in a very true way.

Jakie sat in amazement. I felt that Dadie had mellowed and that he must be a very happy man. But no, it seems he is extremely lonely, feels the lack of grandchildren, finds the hour of waking and the early morning appallingly depressing. He is happier when, after seven or eight cups of tea, he lies in bed reading. Three o'clock in the afternoon is his most difficult time and whisky at six o'clock helps him to continue.

His eyesight is perfect, so he can indulge in his favourite pleasure of reading for the rest of time.

The telephone rang. He answered it in his very poor and small little bedroom with the chamber pot under the wash-basin. 'They've called it off?' he asked; his dinner engagement was off. He would cook eggs or sausages for himself on his 'Little Belling', and he would get through the washing-up and clearing away in ten minutes flat, and then the long evening would be in front of him.

JAMES POPE-HENNESSY

January 25th, 1974

The various news items on the television come and go so rapidly that one wonders at times if one has heard aright. My heart missed a beat as I learnt that James had been severely beaten up, and stabbed. A photograph of James' poetical face was shown on the screen, and before I could take in the horrible fact that he had died as a result of the attack, the news moved on to Ireland or to a football match.

I was struck by an overwhelming sorrow and horror that did not leave me during the night. When I woke and the breakfast tray came in with the newspapers and letters, my hopes that the news-flash might have been a mistake were dashed when I saw the same beautiful face in a photograph on the front page. I looked at my letters. Surely this envelope was written in James' hand? I opened it and a most tender, friendly, sweet letter from him pierced me to the heart. James was thanking me for a present I sent him at Christmas, which he had found on his recent return from America where he had been interviewing friends of Noël Coward for his forthcoming biography, and he longed to meet me again.

James came into my life at the beginning of the last war with a new and fresh sort of appeal. He had 'quality', was intelligent, and intellectual, and serious, and yet good company. I delighted in him, and we became fast friends. We did a book together, he the text and I the photographs, on the bombing of London. Our expeditions to the city were dramatic, often tragic, but agreeable. Sometimes after exploring the still-smoking ruins, we went to the Strand and ate a good lunch in a restaurant.

James introduced me to Clarissa Churchill, who has remained a close friend, and to many others whose company I enjoy.

I remember seeing James from a taxi as he got out of another taxi in front of Batsfords. He was late, he was panicky, his arms full of books. As he descended, his hat hit the top of the taxi, hat and books went flying. I saw in that glimpse myself.

Later James began to be rather difficult. He drank too much. He made friendships too easily with the 'rough trade'. This was dangerous and extremely boring for his other friends, who often said: 'Unless he's lucky, one day James will find himself murdered.' James lost his looks, became bellicose, devilish and impossible. Maybe drugs, as an antidote to drink, did improve the situation. 'You do spread your friendships thin,' he once taunted me. I was hurt. Every time I returned from America I brought him a present. I was always the one to ring first. He seldom took the initiative and then there would be a long silence; and now this.

Reddish: February

The water-garden has become one of the most magical places in the garden. To visit this place of babbling water, and birds, is like being in a different country. To think that all these years I was hardly conscious that a river did go past my property! Every sort of bird seems to congregate here, quite different from those that come to the terrace. We are surprised often to see a heron or two on the lookout for fish. But the greatest excitement is a kingfisher — a rare enough streak of blue, yet suddenly I saw one, and the sight gladdened my fading spirit. Kingfishers fly so quickly that by the time one says 'Look!', they have gone.

This most brilliant metallic bird is said to have such an unpleasant smell for other birds that it is solitary and safe. Then I visited the haunt, a tree by the river, and one day not only did a kingfisher fly past me but it landed on some reeds by the river's edge. Here it stayed a while, then was joined by another one. I am hoping that a family will be hatched in the spring and that they will always stay in the water-garden.

Greatest joy having Dot[13] as a neighbour. She is one of the real characters of which it is said: 'They don't exist any more.'

[13] The Viscountess Head.

Diana Cooper has been spending the weekend and the two crossed swords, but they are both magnanimous and marvellous and appreciate each other. Anne Tree is likewise an oversize personality and character-rorty, Hogarthian and with exquisite understanding of character. It is wonderful to have such friends among the country neighbours, and no need to go to London where there is less time in which to relish at leisure these exceptional, very English types.

Chichicastenango, Guatemala: February

Sam and I admitted that we are not very fond of lakes or mountains! Nevertheless, undaunted, we set off in the beautiful early morning sunlight.

On the road through the mountains, little people, with bundles on their heads, or terrible burdens of earthenware pots and plates strapped to their weary bodies, hurried towards the Sunday market. The hubbub was no less than we expected. We were suddenly involved in a world of wonderful colour, quiet, no evil smells, a beautiful place. The colours were mostly deep dark rose, reds, mauves, purples, blacks, dark browns, dark blues.

The stalls were hung with cloth, handwoven stuffs of brilliant magentas, yellows, blues, purples. They were also selling full-petalled cabbage rose-heads as offerings for the church, and there was an animal market and a food market too. There were women wearing shawls folded on their heads and with fringes hanging down their backs. The older women wore a lot of jewellery. One white-haired old dowager escaped my camera but was magnificent, with more beads than anyone — the *grande dame* of them all.

The Guatemalans, unlike the Mexicans, do not like to sing and dance. They have great dignity, and the bargaining is never a squalid affair. Still it amazed me to see the effort that went in to organizing the stalls, bringing the merchandise from so far and with probably no hope of sales. The tourists behaved badly as usual and were out to be difficult.

At each end of the market are perched the two white churches, twins save that one is Roman Catholic and the other is for the Indians. The former was crowded with people, marriage services being performed and candles being lit. The other church with its poorer carvings was rather like a Renaissance church. Masses of corn cobs and paper dolls were being offered at the shrines and incense blackened everything.

Sam and I collapsed after our long day, and talked of the afterlife, the death of the body but the survival of the spirit. It is against nature that nothing should be carried on. There is growth, wellbeing, life, then death; but, says Sam, it cannot just stop. He is certain that things of the mind are stronger than those of the flesh, and that the great urge, the energy, the knowledge accumulated, must be used up in some other way. Sam has spent much time contemplating, and knows a great deal of the religions and philosophies of the earliest inhabitants of this earth. He ponders much on the mysteries of their civilizations and the future of our own.

I fear that tourism will soon spoil Guatemala; people are finding the place extremely cheap in comparison to their other haunts. Already the merchandise in the city is Americanized. I feel we came here and got out just in time.

THE BERLIN WALL

June 1974

I have just got back from a short visit to the Nico Hendersons. After two days in Bonn staying in the pretty, white icing-sugar Residency, we flew to West Berlin and Ann Fleming and I were taken on a tour of the Wall. It was an experience that was dreadfully disturbing.

The wall itself is depressing enough, a slovenly made slice of foul concrete, too high to scale, with greasy curved top to prevent fleeing hands from getting a hold. Those who take a poor chance on their lives by trying to free themselves from life under the Soviets, have to contend with barbed wire, border guards high in their dreadful turrets, and, worse, guns that go off automatically at a vibration; land mines, potholes and terrible Alsatian dogs that are meagrely fed so that they remain savage.

From our vantage point of safety it was terrible to look upon what appeared to be a completely deserted city. It was as if a scourge had visited the place and life hardly existed. There was nothing to be seen that was free, except a rabbit which darted to and fro among the ruins of what appeared a dead, desiccated and sinister place. Bomb rubble from the Armageddon of the last war was still there; a few distant traffic signals were working, but there was no traffic to be seen, poverty everywhere, hardly any public transport and a foul stench of cheap petrol filled the nostrils.

As it happens, there is, a mile away, one town that though deprived in comparison to West Berlin is very much alive to the theatrical arts. Here stage productions are lavish and there is no shortage of performers, so that when *La Traviata* is done,

211

sixty waiters serve the *demi-monde*. But life in this Russian-dominated 'prison' is tragic and terrifying.

As we were taken to the various checkpoints in our British military car, I was alarmed by the feeling of danger, although there was no need to be. Our guides told us of the frequent attempts at escape that somehow miraculously continue to be successful, though we do not know how many are shot or tortured in their efforts to get away. Those who take on the terrible dare are mostly young, and under interrogation they reveal themselves to have escaped for personal, rather than political reasons. If and when they reach sanctuary, the army gives them a rousing welcome, and the festivity ends in their becoming stupefied with drink. The British Military Police enjoy their job. They love taunting the guards who are court-martialled if they fail to spot and shoot at an escapee; and they and their families may also be tortured. So when the run is on the British fire guns in the air to give the Germans an alibi. To prevent their guards from becoming too friendly, the East Germans change the personnel each day. One man will be unmarried, another will have a family. As strangers they are not likely to exchange confidences. Often the border guards try to escape but then they are shot by their *confrères* fearing retribution.

One of the most 'inviting' spots for a possible get-away is where the river bends, and at a certain point is quite narrow. But this is treacherously deceptive and is heavily defended. Shrines erected to those who have died here are tended carefully with flowers and lamps are renewed. It is a haunting sight.

The hunting down of escapees or smuggling of any sort is unbelievably thorough, yet in spite of this there are still those who have the nerve, or imagination, to overcome *all* difficulties. Close to Checkpoint Charlie there is a small 'museum' containing exhibits which reveal man's ingenuity and courage in his determination to be free.

My greatest hope is that one day during my lifetime the Soviets will crack, that the subjugated satellite countries will regain their freedom. I asked our military guide if he was optimistic. He said: 'Something must change.' Meanwhile he is enjoying his *Boys' Own Annual* fun of helping escapees by 'acts of humanity'; but there is still no crack in the Wall.

A TIME FOR REFLECTION

March 13th, 1974

Yesterday I went to the Imperial War Museum, not my favourite place, to see the collection of photographs that I had taken during the war for the Ministry of Information. They have all been put into over thirty albums and, to my amazement, I find there are thirty or forty thousand of them.

It was an extraordinary experience to relive those war years; so much of it had been forgotten, and most of the people are now dead; the Western Front, where at least three hundred of my pictures were unaccountably lost, Burma, India, China. It was fascinating to see the scenes in old Imperial Simla, the rickshaws drawn by uniformed servants, the grandeur of the houses, the palaces; the bar scenes, the men on leave swigging beer, and to wonder how I had been able to 'frat' with such unfamiliar types. I had not realized that I had taken so many documentary pictures, and that such a lot were only of technical interest. Looking at them today, I saw many ideas that are now 'accepted', but which, thirty years ago, were before their time. The sheer amount of work I had done confounded me. In spite of the horror of the war, much of it had taken me to places of beautiful natural landscapes.

It was a thrilling but upsetting morning, for I felt that I was dead and that people were speaking of me in the past. 'The greatest collection by one person of any subject in our museum.'

After three hours of deep concentration, I got up from the desk to prepare myself to go home and to leave the completely different world I had been in.

I went out into the grey dreariness of Lambeth today. It had been a particularly revolting week with strikes, power cuts and epidemics. Despite the dark grey skies I was buoyant and would not believe that my life had lost any of its old fire and zest. Much depended on the future.

A NOTE TO THE READER

If you have enjoyed Cecil Beaton's Memoir enough to leave a review on **Amazon** and **Goodreads**, then we would be truly grateful.

Sapere Books is an exciting new publisher of brilliant fiction and popular history.

To find out more about our latest releases and our monthly bargain books visit our website: **saperebooks.com**

49404794R00131

Made in the USA
Columbia, SC
20 January 2019